# PROTECTING CHILDREN FROM CHILD PROTECTIVE SERVICES

By

## ALAN L. SCHWARTZ

First published by AuthorHouse 04/19/04

ISBN: 1-4140-5563-3 (e-book)
ISBN: 1-4184-3703-4 (Paperback)

Library of Congress Control Number: 2003099858


This book is printed on acid free paper.


Printed in the United States of America
Bloomington, IN

# TABLE OF CONTENTS

# PREFACE

Having had aspirations of teaching and counseling high school students, I found similar satisfaction counseling high school dropouts in redirecting their lives by obtaining a GED, completing vocational training, securing employment and successfully raising their own family. My employment in several different state programs assisting families through difficult times provided me with a unique perspective of the inherent goodness in people and the incongruities plaguing state agencies in providing humane and supportive services to the public. My philosophy of working with people may be considered an anathema to program administrators, but I would not have survived thirty years in the Social Service field had it not been for the support from my co-workers as well as the families and children I had the pleasure of knowing and serving.

Currently federal investigators are evaluating Child Protective Services nationwide. Of forty-five states tested, not one has passed. There are good reasons for their failure. It is easy for CPS to point the finger of blame at parents, but CPS has a poor record of protecting children and providing appropriate services to return children to family in a timely manner. One director of a state Department of Children and Family Services stated he expected his CPS agency to fail the federal test in several areas. The areas included a lack of focus toward reuniting families because the system leans more toward adoption, an overrepresentation of black children in the agency's care, and the need to improve substance abuse and mental health services

On the surface this sounds good but he is the director of the "system". His system has also come under scrutiny for losing hundreds of children. He admits to having no apprehension about the entire (evaluation) process. By stating the system leans toward adoption, he is either stating he is not in control of his own program or family reunification is not the focus of his program. This indicates his first choice is not to return children in a timely manner or to find alternative placement with extended family. His reference to an overrepresentation of black children indicates he is blaming black parents for ineffective parenting. Is this a matter of education or are drugs at the center of this problem? Improving substance abuse and mental health services puts the problem at the doorstep of another agency. Most of the other forty-four directors might recite similar reasons for failing the federal test. The federal government grants almost ten billion dollars to states. The main problem is quality of service not funding.

Reading this book will dispel some of the CPS myths and offer insight as to the workings of CPS and the Juvenile Court. Case studies will be presented and alternative programs suggested to relieve the over-burdened Workers and allow them to focus on the children truly needing services. For those studying to become Social Workers, this book will prepare you to assist CPS clients achieve stability in their lives and offer personal insights not found in textbooks.

A father put duct tape over his daughter's mouth because she talked back to him and used some language that pushed his buttons. The daughter was removed and spent two years in a paid foster home placement. Once bi-weekly she would have a supervised visit with her father, step-mother and baby brother. The father's attorney appealed the removal of the child to a higher court and the removal was overturned. Now the Juvenile Court Judge was concerned with how to reunify the girl because she had bonded with the foster family. That never seems to be important when children are removed from their home. The girl was still bonded to her father. Had the judge invited the child and her attorney into chambers, he could have asked her directly how she felt about going back home. He would have had his answer. The child missed two years of watching her brother grow up and her brother missed two years of having an older sister.

There is no doubt child abuse and neglect exist and rob children of an emotionally and physically stabilizing childhood; however, approximately 30% of each caseload represents cases lacking the standard of ongoing abuse necessary for removing children for a substantial period of time. Leaving this child in the home would not have brought about her imminent death but would have protected her from languishing in an out-of-home setting longer than she needed.

In 1978 the U.S. Congress was pressed to pass the Indian Child Welfare Act after hearing congressional testimony of Native American children removed from family and reservation by church missionaries who wanted to protect the children from poverty by adopting these children out to their church members spread across the country. There was no way for these children to ever find their way back home. No records were saved or allowed to be opened. Occasionally we still hear miraculous stories of these now young adults reuniting with their family by tracing them through the Internet.

It is time for the U.S. Congress to investigate the services provided children and families by state CPS as it did with the Native American children. Families no longer view CPS as a resource in times of stress. Each county or

CPS jurisdiction is different in its approach to child welfare services. Even in the same jurisdiction there is little agreement in arriving at a uniformly accepted and objective definition of what constitutes child abuse. There needs to be conformity to one standard of operation and services that will do justice to family and children. Can you define child abuse and get a stranger to agree with your definition? In appraising services to families, a good starting point might be the Indian Child Welfare Act.

It is important to understand that abused children will treat their children the same way they were treated as children, especially when they encounter stressful periods in their lives. For example, when a child pushes his father's buttons repeatedly, tension mounts in the father. The resultant lashing out by the father is more dependent on the father's personality and the manner in which he was raised rather than a premeditated desire to hurt his child. For this reason we must teach families and children conflict resolution and problem solving techniques. This is best done in the home with the family intact. I am a strong advocate for in-home counseling programs because one hour each week in a counselor's office does not compare to a team of counselors in the home on a daily basis if needed and carrying cell phones for emergency situations. The family is more apt to function "normally" at home versus an office. Because of the intensity, services can be completed successfully in a shorter period of time. It seems probable children will love and nurture their own children if they come from a family that has learned to work together harmoniously.

In this book, my use of the masculine form in referring to a child's caretaker and professionals in the various agencies is done for expediency purposes only. Also the use of Social Worker, Case Manager and Worker are interchangeable. It is encouraging to see fathers stepping in to take custody of their children from Juvenile Courts. I encourage middle schools and CPS work together to teach boys and girls parenting skills, the importance of the father's relationship with his children and the hazards to be avoided in the role of step-parents. Unless these lessons are taught to middle school young people, they may not be learned anywhere else. I found many young families waiting too long to seek help because they didn't know where to go or that the needed services were even available.

I welcome hearing from those impacted by CPS, foster care and the Juvenile Court. How did your experience with CPS affect your life? Did you have adequate legal representation? For young people, did your attorney meet with you to present your wishes to the judge? Your account is imperative to advocate for appropriate changes to CPS and the Juvenile Court to better serve families in the future. If you are willing to consent to an interview for this research, please let me know. You may reach me either at: Schwartz@theramp.net or at P.O. Box 943, Rock Falls, IL. 61071-0943.

# INTRODUCTION

In the early 1950's Child Protective Services was in its infancy. Social Workers had a hands-on relationship with families. They were more involved with truancy and chastising children for putting firecrackers in mailboxes, than investigating the kind of abuse cases we see today. Before automobiles got faster and families began to make their way to the suburbs, children still respected and feared (loved) their parents and wanted to be like their heroes and role models. If children broke the law, they feared the consequences. A teacher once told me that as a child, if he didn't have his homework done, his teacher would rap him over the knuckles with a ruler. He didn't dare tell his father for fear his father would mete out a more severe punishment.

The advent of the sixties brought a gradual but steady decline in children's respect for their parents, authority figures and the law. Technology was beginning giant leaps forward and there was no turning back. With both parents now working longer hours, television, drug and alcohol addiction, divorce and the extended family moving away in different directions, children gravitated to interests outside the home. Peer group influence became more important to children than the wishes of parents. As a result parents began to lose control of their children.

Today the problems are more complex. Children are not only tuning out their parents and authority figures, they are talking back disrespectfully and demonstrating a disdain for parents and the laws of society. There is chaos in the classroom. Our probation departments are stressed with an increasing number of teenagers committing more violent crimes than ever before. Drug experimentation and other risky behavior are expected to increase causing tremendous pressures on parents and law enforcement agencies. The role models of yesterday are no longer. It is not helpful that athletes and people having the credentials to be role models are in the public eye for their illegal or immoral exploits without seeming to suffer consequences for their actions. Parents use drugs and alcohol while preaching the gospel of do as I say, not as I do. Children are exposed to this dichotomy from early childhood. The explosion of technology will continue to weaken the preponderance of family. Now children begin their quest for independence before they are ready. Many parents realize the mistakes they made earlier in their lives. Parents grapple with holding their child back from making the same mistakes they did and feel they have to resort to force in protecting their child from exercising his perceived right to independence from the structures that should be the cornerstones of his life. Although it is too late to right the ship, should CPS be in charge of policing these children? Empathy and understanding need to be brought back into the framework of CPS services. We need to blame parents less and support them more. There should be nothing wrong in reaching out to parents in the 30% category with a sense of love, hope and education for a better future.

As the changes to society began to escalate, CPS found themselves in the role of catch-up. As child abuse referrals to CPS began to escalate, CPS moved from a resource for families to a more punitive relationship. Attorneys-General have become overly vindictive in their pursuit of severance and adoption rather than reunification. The child's wishes are not taken into consideration. To the Attorney-General, adoption seems the only goal. The problem of course is adoptive homes are not available for too many of these children. These "professionals" do not think twice about the children as they put another notch in their belt.

The emotional involvement of Social Workers with families and children has weakened as they have had to labor under ever-increasing paperwork, low wages and increasing responsibilities of accountability to society's expectations of protecting children. Social Workers have become Case Managers. Instead of an emotional involvement the Worker is expected by administrators to act as the hub of a wheel and farm out family services to other agencies and wait for reports to come in as to the family's progress toward reunification. A byproduct of this approach is CPS does not have to be alone in answering criticism of its handling of a case. The goal of CPS is not to attract negative media attention. This hangs over the Worker's head all the time and precludes sincere efforts to reunify families.

Once a parent agrees to a Dependency Petition, he loses control of his child. The CPS administration fears liability if the parent has input into his child's care and the child suffers injury. As a result the Case Manager takes over full responsibility in making decisions regarding the child's physical and emotional needs. Even the parent's consent to major surgery is a formality. The Case Manager answers only to his superiors and the "professionals" affiliated with the case. Neither the family nor the child has any involvement with these decisions. As a result the number of children in foster care can be expected to climb over the 600,000 mark and will continue to rise. The older the child is, the harder to find an adoptive home. Children are not easily adopted over the age of three. At preschool age we can expect behavior problems to emerge in children. So much depends on inherited genetics. If parents have a history of drug addiction, the child may begin to show disorders of Attention Deficit or a greater susceptibility to drug usage than other children. One child had severe Diabetes, ADD and was manic depressive. Fortunately his step-father took him in. If children are not returned home and they are too old to be adopted, they are certain to languish in an out-of-home placement facility. Even worse is the periodic change in placement which cannot be avoided unless other options are considered. Extended family is a viable option but too often discounted by CPS out of fear the biological parent may have unauthorized contact with his child or disrupt the placement. Instead of paying an adoption subsidy to strangers, why not pay it to an extended family? Most of the time extended family is not considered because the administration does not want to go out looking for the family or spend the time completing home studies and certifying the extended family for adoption.

When I was working on the reservation, an adoptive parent and her thirteen year old adoptive daughter came in for assistance in finding the young lady's biological mother. The drug-addicted mother had burned her infant daughter on a stove. After an extensive search extended family was located and they welcomed the chance to meet their niece. These were relatives employed by police departments. The young lady met her mother and was satisfied, but now she had discovered a whole new world of family members concerned about her welfare and would be available if she would ever need assistance.

# CHAPTER ONE

# THE CHILD PROTECTIVE SERVICES PROCESS

The mission of Child Protective Services is to protect children from abuse and to provide appropriate services to keep families intact. This seems to be a perfectly acceptable definition to follow; yet, it lacks an objective and verifiable means of testing for abuse and leaves each case referred to CPS open to interpretation. Although each CPS jurisdiction has formulated a similar definition of child abuse, the definition is not juxtaposed against each case referred to

1

CPS and leaves abuse open to interpretation. It is similar to Chief Justice Potter Stewart's definition of hard-core pornography: "I know it when I see it". Each person phoning CPS with a suspicion of child abuse believes abuse is occurring and needs immediate intervention. Through public announcements CPS encourages the public to phone in any suspicion of abuse and the anonymity of the caller is promised. The mere anonymity and the protection from having to testify in court emboldens many callers to overstate the abuse in order to secure the child's removal. Removal becomes the goal of the caller and woe unto CPS if the child is not removed. Too often the threat of negative media attention is the driving force in a child's ultimate removal.

Professionals as well as neighbors and relatives allow themselves to get swept up in making allegations of abuse to CPS based on subjective interpretation of what they see, hear or believe. Elian Gonzalez was a case in point. Everything in this case was subjective except the biological father's wanting his son returned to him. Everyone had a cause in this melee. Whether Elian remained in the United

States or returned to Cuba made no difference. Similarly children removed by CPS languish in an out-of-home placement and are forgotten. It is newsworthy for only the moment.

Several myths permeate CPS and are effectively used by CPS to generate support. These are "feel-good" myths. People feel good toward preserving what supports their perception of children as honest with a child-like naivete. One myth is: "Children don't lie". But they do lie and they become quite good at it. Young children will lie out of fear of authority figures. They are frightened into making up stories or telling lies to get off the hook. If questioned the child will give the answer he thinks the interrogator wants to hear. Children use a lie to protect themselves from punishment they might deserve, for getting someone into trouble, and finally to shift attention away from themselves. When a teacher asks a child to explain how his leg got bruised, he is perceptive enough to read the level of concern in the teacher's voice. If the child is taken to the principal's office with the teacher, it can be even more traumatic to the child. A child might say his mother did it because he

3

doesn't want to confess to climbing a tree his mother told him to avoid. A child might also believe the interrogator would believe that if his mother did it, it would be ok. It is amazing how something as minor as this will escalate into a substantiation of abuse. Children are exposed to lies from very early in life, and we all enjoy listening to a child's imagination at work. If a child tells the authority figure what the person wants to hear, he learns the interrogation will stop and he can go back to play.

An elementary school teacher saw a burn mark on a Native American child's abdomen area, CPS was phoned and the child was placed in foster care. The investigator went to the cramped motel room where the mother lived with her boyfriend to find the curling iron he believed was used by the boyfriend to punish the child. When he could not find the curling iron he confiscated an iron. Now let's put the puzzle together. Obviously the boyfriend wanted to harm the child. Either he was ironing at the time or he found the iron and decided to heat it up enough to burn the child. When the iron was hot enough he raised the child's shirt and burned him in that one spot. Obviously the child did not struggle. There was no indication of fear in the child toward his mother's friend. What we did determine is that the child played on monkey bars on the playground. The monkey bars had been exposed to 100+ degree days. We returned the child and no further problem occurred. In fact the mother later referred a family member for services.

Another CPS myth is: "We err on the side of protecting the child", which has become the standard response to cover mistakes. How can anyone argue against such a virtuous statement? CPS mistakes occur by not taking time to adequately investigate an allegation of abuse. It is far easier to let the court decide the case than leave the child in the home and face negative media attention if the wrong decision were made. The statement itself admits to an error by CPS and informs the listener that these errors in judgment will continue to be made and should continue to be justified.

Errors are acceptable because we are trying to protect children and we cannot always be right in what we are doing. CPS will not admit to mistakes, nor will CPS learn from mistakes. This is not acceptable.

Two young elementary school sisters told their teacher that two illegal male immigrants were staying at their house and the men would watch them through their window at night. Without talking to the parents, CPS removed the children from school and placed them in foster care on a failure to protect petition in Juvenile Court. When the parents came to my office, the father told me he had gone outside at night to catch the young men in the act. When they didn't come out he put his 2x4 down until the next night. Unfortunately CPS got involved the next day. Had CPS talked to the parents they would have learned the family was staying at the home of the grandmother, the family did not have the resources to move out, and it had been the grandmother's decision to let the men stay at her home.

Another CPS myth is teens are abused by their parents and will behave appropriately once removed. These cases involve teenagers who are testing their independence by acting out at home, school and/or the community. The parent becomes frustrated and abuses the child. Unless necessary and based on evidence of long-term abuse, the removal of the child from his home frequently causes the parent to lose his authority and power over his child and emboldens the child to challenge his parent when he is returned. Unfortunately CPS is not willing to admit a mistake. The nightmare for CPS begins by removing a teen without adequate justification, i.e., no long-term abuse present but escalating because of the friction between parent and child. The teen usually does not change but progressively worsens the longer he remains out of the home. Rather than re-evaluating policy, CPS continues to remove recalcitrant teens from family. A teen has no bond toward the system that removed him; consequently, he will not listen to his CPS Worker or the Juvenile Court Judge. Often these young people are dually-adjudicated as a dependent minor and a juvenile delinquent. This routinely happens to boys but girls are quickly closing the gap. This category of teen passes from foster home, to shelter, to detention and finally to therapeutic group home. Along the way they learn from one another how to beat the system and the game of us against them is on. These teens do not face severe penalties because lock-up facilities are overcrowded.

The financial cost to taxpayers is substantial. Once the teens turn eighteen and are out of the system, family stands ready to take them back but the child is now obligated to cooperate with his parent or find another place to live. The same result could have been achieved without removing the teen, also known as a tough love approach.

There is nothing scientific or rational about a CPS investigation and/or services provided the family. With the exception of medically proven abuse of a child, the referrals and investigations rely on subjective evaluations of abuse. The services supplied the family represent a cookie cutter approach, which is formulated on what looks good to the Juvenile Court and what is offered by the budget. No one knows for certain these services fit the individual needs of the family or that the family will continue to effectively manage stress in their family after reunification. These doubts delay or prevent reunification in a timely manner. The pervading fear of reputations being ruined by returning a child to further abuse from the same parent permeates everyone connected with the case and effectively precludes a timely return. Once the label of "abusive" has been placed on a person it is hard to remove or trust that person. Gradually the case plan turns from reunification to long-term foster care. The vagaries of life do not subside because the child is out of the home, except now the family is under a microscope. CPS will make a big issue if the parent stumbles along the way. Divorce, illness, financial problems, a new partner, and a host of other changes in circumstances may have been absorbed by an intact family but now become severe obstacles to reunification. How can the parent be ready for reunification if he cannot keep a job, pick the right mate, handle expenses, or find better housing. Many CPS agencies now require Workers to write one case plan for reunification and another for severance of parental rights even though the original allegation was not so severe as to warrant severance. With each six month court review the Worker submits a Progress Report. If the Worker pounces on each set-back of the parent, he can easily make that seem as justification to delay reunification. Losing a job is an example, but a job has nothing to do with effective parenting. The parent might receive Unemployment

Insurance but that is not necessarily considered by the Worker.

The journey to reunification takes precedence over the original allegation. Perception is everything. Actually most Workers do not even recall the original allegation because the case transfers from Worker to Worker so frequently. The new Worker reads a transfer summary when he should read the entire file. By reading the entire file a previously hidden notation might jump out and spark a fresh and untried tack to achieve reunification or placement with a member of the extended family. It is not unusual to place a child in foster care and later discover a pre-existing and undiagnosed medical problem of the parent or child caused the original problem between parent and child. It takes a strong and conscientious professional to get that medical impairment diagnosed, to convince administration to accept it as the cause of ineffective parenting, and then to get the case plan changed and approved by all of the professionals. Connecting the dots or admitting a mistake are two areas CPS is too often not willing to consider. Their income from their job is too important.

Generally an allegation of child abuse or neglect is received from an anonymous caller to the CPS Hotline, which assigns the case to an investigator in the CPS Intake Unit. If referrals are received 24/7, they are prioritized depending on the severity of the allegation. Cases emanating from law enforcement, medical personnel and educators carry the highest priority. The Intake Unit determines the validity of the allegation. If the investigator finds enough evidence of family dysfunction to cause concern, he will plug in CPS funded programs to keep the family intact. If the evidence warrants, he may remove the child by filing a Dependency Petition with the Juvenile Court. The Dependency Petition cites the allegation made to CPS, what was uncovered through the investigation, and why the investigator believes the best interest of the minor dictates the child's removal from the home. Usually the investigator makes the decision in consultation with his supervisor and the state Attorney-General's office. In making the decision to file a Dependency Petition, too much credence is given to the source of the allegation, consideration to potential publicity should the child not be removed and pressures of time restraints hampering completion of a full investigation before the parent might become alarmed and hide the child. Removing a child and filing a Dependency Petition sends the case to Juvenile Court, relieves time pressures and protects CPS. Rightly or wrongly, CPS is protected because the child is now out of the home. Remember CPS errs on the side of protecting children, which absolves them from criticism. No one ever challenges a removal.

Fear of bad publicity causes an overload on the CPS Worker, in that support for the Worker to reunify the family is often lacking. The lack of support can be traced from the immediate supervisors up through the administrators. It is an unexpressed concern that abuse might be renewed should the child remain with the parent or returned to him. Timely reunification should be the focus of CPS but the mind-set of the immediate supervisor, administrators and personnel reviewing CPS cases is to over-emphasize the factors supporting continued separation rather than the factors supporting reunification.

CPS Workers are not promoted to supervisors unless they demonstrate caution in their own cases. Again this caution does not apply to drug addiction or verifiable long-term abuse by parents. It applies to the marginal cases where the original allegations do not support long-term separation of children from their biological family. As happens so often, the original allegation gets lost to the process. Areas not even related to the original allegation are over-emphasized to substantiate a decision not to reunify. Reunification is also delayed through the lack of qualified attorneys representing the parent and child. Attorneys do not attend any case staffing to lodge a complaint if proposed services are not justified. A case staffing is held to review the progress of the family. Invariably the family is viewed as not making significant progress. Lacking any support for reunification, the Worker loses his desire and motivation. Neither does CPS adhere to granting reunification should the parent complete specific goals. As caseloads grow, so does Worker attrition. The case remains stagnant and eventually receives less attention from the Worker. A Worker cannot maintain a high degree of involvement when there is no enthusiasm for the reunification. The Worker is not unlike the parent. Each needs a pat on the back, a recognition of the positives, and hope for the future.

The case staffing can be an effective tool to help the Case Manager in reaching a decision on how to proceed with a case. Frequently staffings are held to crisis manage a foster child blowing yet another placement. The Juvenile Court Probation uses them to determine the most appropriate placement for a delinquent teen. The expertise of psychologists, medical personnel, family and the Case Manager still does not insure success. The staffing is usually used as a court of last resort. I remember attending a staffing of two teen sisters who needed to be evaluated after blowing another placement. This time they would go to a highly structured group home. I was told they disliked each other and could not get along together. They sat on a couch in the waiting room. One of the girls was drinking a soda. She instinctively handed it to her sister who took a sip and handed it back. Today I would not be surprised if they were still together. The "professionals" were in the adjoining office oblivious to the soda incident or possibly that the hatred statement in the file might not be fully accurate. Many life-altering decisions are made from inaccurate information. In an effort to learn how to improve services and assessments, many states are opening their case files. By volunteering to open files, CPS programs will benefit and improve their programs. Mistakes by CPS need not continue at the levels currently hidden in their archives. More money to fix the system is not the problem. The services cannot be improved through secrecy or under the guise of protecting confidentiality.

When a child is removed, the parent is not but should be consulted in regard to placement with extended family. In most cases CPS has an adversarial relationship with the parent. It is not uncommon for this mistrust to carry over to grandparents and close family members. Indeed it is near impossible for relatives to even get information as to where the Social Worker is located. CPS is not adverse to relocating its offices periodically. These Workers and CPS offices are not usually found in the phone book. Many offices are now under tight security. There is a reason these offices are under tight security. In removing children from their home and placing children in shelter or foster home, Workers have become insensitive to the needs of the child and the parent. The placement serves the administration's needs first, but the Worker is viewed by family as insensitive to the family's needs. Often grandparents are seen to be as culpable as the parent. Social Workers do not start out this way. It comes from the top down. It is impressed on Workers to not jeopardize winning the court case. Winning the court case depends on keeping the child from parents and family members at least until the Dependency Petition is agreed to by the parent. The less family contact with the child, the less he will say to family. The less family knows; the less of an obstacle to CPS winning the case. Relatives do not aggressively seek out information, because they do not know whom or what to believe. It does not mean they are not willing to help in the investigation or placement phase. The Juvenile Court Judge, attorneys and counselors are protected from witnessing first hand the child's trauma in losing his home and his parents. Very young children will agonize that their parent is not there when they go to bed or when they awaken in the morning. The state salaried psychologists will evaluate a parent but not a parent and child together. If the psychologist does not include the relationship of parent and child together in his report, neither the attorney nor the judge has any idea of the child's bond with his parent. No assessment of the child's bond with his parent is ever mentioned in many court reports. A foster parent reports the child wets the bed after a visit and believes the parent traumatized the child during the visit. These unjustified reports are made frequently as foster parents become invested in what they believe is the best interest of the child - not to return home. Children are truly amazing in their ability to adapt. They size up the foster home quickly and acclimate themselves to their new environment. Meanwhile the foster parent is bonding with the child and believes the child is bonding to the foster family.

One such case involved a Native American seven year old boy, whose drug addicted mother disappeared after her child was placed in a foster home by CPS. Desiring to adopt the child, the foster parents hired an attorney. The attorney fought my recommendation of placing the child with extended family on a reservation. Similar to the missionaries, the attorney cited the poor economic conditions the boy would face in going to a reservation (Sound like Elian Gonzalez?) and family with whom he had had very little contact. The Juvenile Court judge ruled in favor of adoption by the foster parents. When the child reached high school he developed suicidal ideations. When the adoptive parents ran out of insurance coverage for the child's hospital stay, they contacted CPS for help. As luck would have it, I overheard the psychologist talking about the boy. Through contact with the relatives on the reservation it was learned the family still wanted the child, the mother had recovered from her drug addiction, was living on the reservation and in the middle of exhibiting her art. She came back, had dinner with the adoptive parents and took her son back with her. Ironically the same judge ruling against placement with relatives restored the parental rights to the biological mother. Did he give any thought to his role in ruling against placement with family and the child's subsequent suicidal ideation? Why did the child's attorney not investigate placement with relatives? Even had he not agreed with my recommendation, at least he would have earned his income by adequately representing the child.

These cases are often considered as isolated cases but they are not. Another Native American teen in long-term foster care with state CPS and living with a Caucasian family wrapped up his belongings and stood in front of a train. Only Congressional Hearings can rectify these mistakes by requiring CPS put the best interest of the child first. This can only be done by setting standards for investigation, removal of children and subsequent placement of children. A review of cases will support the need for exit interviews for families and children experiencing foster care placement. The child's attorney should be required to observe one entire visit between parent and child. Fortunately one of the two children cited above lived but not through any efforts by CPS, the Juvenile Court or the child's attorney. It is not an example of professionals working in the best interest of the child. As Congress learned in gathering evidence that resulted in the Indian Child Welfare Act, this is just the tip of the problem.

## PROTECTING CHILDREN FROM CHILD PROTECTIVE SERVICES

If CPS and its supporters have any influence, the current federal investigation of CPS will be set aside and CPS will return to business as usual. Too many professionals derive a substantial income from CPS cases and the money is acquired without having to adequately represent their client.

Investigating an allegation of child abuse/neglect is a time-consuming and emotionally draining task. If the investigator decides the case should go to the Juvenile Court, he staffs the case with the state Attorney-General representing CPS, prepares an Initial Court Report and presents the case at the first judiciary hearing. Next he will serve a Temporary Custody Notice to the parent or adult in charge of the child at the time he removes the child. He must gather clothing for the child, file for medical and dental coverage, obtain school transfer papers and provide pertinent background information to the foster family. As you might expect, little time exists between the initial investigation and the removal of the child. Certainly no time to do an in-depth investigation. This is also where CPS investigators are prone to make mistakes. If two investigators were on the same case, one could continue gathering evidence by talking to relatives, medical personnel and neighbors. The second investigator might even talk to the parent. To remove the child in a secretive manner suggests CPS is afraid the parent might talk his way out of the removal. In the 30% category parents should be given the chance to explain how the incident occurred. The investigation itself is effective in sending a strong message to a parent. The case then could be referred to a non-court (family preservation) caseload to be monitored for a period of time and work with the family in providing appropriate services to resolve the original allegation and close the case.

For those investigations requiring the filing of a Dependency Petition, the case is now ready for transfer to the Ongoing Unit, which is responsible for guiding the family to reunification. Cases involving drug addiction constitute an overwhelming percentage of failures to achieve reunification. CPS should open its files on these families and hold public discussions on how to better handle them. The effects of using meth-amphetamines are now becoming well-known to the public. A father was parked on the interstate when he beheaded his son. He was found to have used meth that day. Parents on this drug have been found to do horrendous things to their children. It does not matter if the parent had no expectation the drug would have this effect on him. New drugs are continually appearing and even taking the first hit will cause an immediate addiction and violence.

Changes in law now require parents to complete their required treatment in one to two years. This may have been instituted as a response to the increase in drug addicted parents failing to reunify and other cases taking several years to achieve reunification. Today the clock starts ticking at the Initial Court Hearing, where an attorney is appointed by the judge to represent the child. If the parents are financially eligible, an attorney is also appointed to represent them. Attorneys are appointed at county expense when parents are financially qualified.

From the initial hearing to the second usually takes a few weeks. Theoretically the attorneys will have met with their clients before the second hearing. It is rare indeed to find an attorney who has met with his client before the second hearing. This is a disservice to the parent and child as CPS will use these weeks to put pressure on the parent to plead guilty to the Dependency Petition. These meetings with the parent are usually conducted with no attorney present although one was appointed.

By removing the child from the home with the Temporary Custody Notice signed by a Judge of the Juvenile Court, CPS now has the leverage to strike a bargain with the parent. Under the guise of wanting to help the family achieve reunification, CPS and the Attorney-General will offer to modify the Dependency Petition provided the parent admits to the petition. To the naïve parent everything seems rosy. The parent believes an anonymous person made the allegation, but these nice people at CPS want to help me, an attorney has been appointed to represent me in court and even my child will have an attorney who will tell the court how much my child wants to return home. Once CPS achieves the Dependency Petition the parent has lost all hope of maintaining any control of his child's life. The parent will only be consulted if his child requires a major operation.

Once the parent agrees to the petition, the screws are tightened. The Ongoing Worker will devise a litany of programs to frustrate a parent so much as to jeopardize his successful completion of reunification. At each visit the parent must accept the physical and emotional changes in his child, knowing that he has no control to even request a certain style of haircut.

Without consultation with the parent's attorney, the parent may be required to submit to a psychological evaluation with a CPS salaried psychologist. The psychologist has access to the CPS file (the CPS point of view), with information compiled by the CPS investigator. It is too easy for the psychologist to slant his report in favor of CPS. One young lady had allowed her four year old son to roam the apartment complex relatively unsupervised. The allegation was phoned in to the CPS Intake Unit and the child was placed in foster care. As a requirement of the reunification plan she submitted to a psychological evaluation with the CPS funded psychologist. Half-way through the interview she stormed out of the office upset the psychologist suggested she should improve her class of friends. The young lady had been on her own for a substantial period of time and she desired to inculcate that sense of independence in her son. There was no mention of possible abuse of the child in the original allegation. The supposition that the mother's behavior would contribute to some harm to the child shows the use of subjectivity in current allegations and the subsequent removal of children. This was a head-strong young lady who stood up to CPS and for her desire to raise her child the way she saw fit. Should she be allowed to parent her child or must she conform to prevailing beliefs of effective parenting practice? Unless she was willing to admit she was wrong, she could not expect to get her son back. It might have been interesting to have evaluated the child to determine his level of maturity and sophistication. The psychologist might have extended the evaluation to include the child separately from his mother, followed by one with both of them together.

Another reason for CPS to open its files is to evaluate whether contracting a psychological evaluation is just and fair to family and children. It is virtually impossible to find any redeeming qualities in a parent from reading these evaluations. A psychologist has a vested interest in slanting his report if he is paid by the state. The psychologist must also protect his reputation from the possibility a child may be injured if he recommends a return to parent. How about allowing a parent to select his own psychologist and not provide any information from the CPS file to the psychologist? The parent might frame the allegation into a request for suggestions on how to resolve the concerns expressed in the allegations. The recommendations of the psychologist would be used by CPS in its case plan submitted to the court. During some of my readings I found myself wondering why I could not find any positives about the parent or any assessment of the strength of the bond between the parent and the child. The evaluation certainly did not agree with my assessment of the parent.

Once the Dependency Petition is accepted by the Juvenile Court, the Ongoing Worker devises programs that follow a cookie cutter approach to treatment. The budget dictates the treatment programs. These treatment programs are prescribed to weaken a parent's resolve to fight for his child. The treatment program is placed in the case plan and is approved by the judge and may even be approved by the parent as a "contract" enabling CPS to recommend reunification to the court if the parent completes treatment successfully. The case plan might pick from a variety of programs: state funded counseling, anger management classes, drug and alcohol testing, supervised visits between parent and child in neutral locations, parent effectiveness training, vocational stability, marital counseling and domestic violence counseling. Counseling sessions involve one hour each week and it is no wonder substantial progress is not achieved. Would four hours of counseling each week be more productive? Whoever figured out that removing a child from his home and parent only needed one hour each week. Other options need to be tried. Reunification cannot be achieved in a timely manner if these methods are continued. Again the counseling is a state funded program. The whole CPS and Juvenile Court process is so demeaning that most services provided to change behavior in a parent are redundant.

The Worker might require a one hour weekly or bi-weekly supervised visit between parent and child.

Supervised visits are to prevent the parent from absconding with his child, saying something to disrupt the child, or eliciting some information from the child that might jeopardize his welfare.

In Chicago there was a mother who tricked the person supervising her visit with her son to jump in a waiting car and take off. Why would she do this?

The person who supervises a visit is usually paid to transport the child to the visit site, to remain in listening distance, to return the child to the foster home and to write a detailed report.

The court-approved case plan may even require random drug and alcohol testing of the parent. One parent agreed to the random tests until one day he was helping fix a car and drank a beer. You guessed it. That one beer was enough to drag the court hearings on for a longer period of time. If the alcohol is the problem, let's focus on that. If not leave it alone. No evidence was presented to connect the father to drugs or alcohol; the mother did have a DUI. No children were with her at the time of the infraction. The children were old enough not to be at risk if the father had a beer.

Should cases such as this tie-up a court calendar and supportive services to make home visits, secure drug tests and transport the family to counseling and court hearings?

The case plan must be simple and to the point. Case plans become all inclusive of treatment programs designed to satisfy the Juvenile Court. The longer a child remains in foster care, the more difficult it becomes to restore the family. Families will grow in a different direction from their child in foster care. When the child returns from foster care, he may try to bring his family back to where it was when he left. To him, his dysfunctional family was normal. He knew how to act in that setting. Now it feels strange, confusing, and uncomfortable. Unable to comprehend the changes to his family, the child begins to act out and further counseling is needed to resolve these problems.

# CHAPTER TWO

# A CASE STUDY

"All I wanted was for our family to be fixed and put back together again. If I had known this would happen, I never would have said anything". These words were spoken by a sixteen year old young man who felt his father needed counseling to put his mind back on the right track. He understood he and his sister would be removed from the home and eventually reunited with their parents. What he learned was no one wanted to listen to him and decisions regarding him and his sister would be made without their input. He and his sister were shipped some 1000 miles away from their home to live with "relatives" in another state.

When I contacted him he had already figured out his family would not be reunited in spite of his father's counselor reporting to the court that the father and mother were ready for reunification after having completed one year of counseling. The counselor was in private practice and for some reason his recommendation was not accepted by CPS and the AG. Although the case had been in the Juvenile Court for one year, the young man told me he had not even heard he had an attorney and no attorney had contacted him. Neither had he been contacted by any Social Worker. I was the first one. He felt he and his sister had been victimized by the system. The young man was on his high school football team and both of the children were attaining good grades. He and his sister loved their father and mother and felt no fear of harm from either of them. The young man was remarkable in that he had a better understanding of the problem facing his family than all the "professionals" put together.

It was because of young people such as these that I developed a philosophy of listening to young people and they will direct you to the right decision regarding their future. One also needs to sit in the family's living room to truly understand the family. This is why in-home counseling is more effective than weekly one hour counseling sessions or requiring parents to come to the CPS office. The most effective teachers are the ones who make home visits. If the child sees his teacher laughing and joking with his parents, he becomes a member of the team without realizing it.

The interesting aspect of this case is the children's placement out-of-state was in violation of CPS policy and procedure as well as circumventing the Interstate Compact for the Placement of Children (ICPC). The ICPC is the first step in placing children out of one jurisdiction into another. The sending state must seek approval of the receiving state and a commitment of the receiving state to furnish progress reports on the children. The receiving state provides a home study of the family with whom the children will reside. All family members over the age of eighteen need to submit to a background check and proof of relationship between the families will be verified. CPS did not apply to ICPC before sending the children to what was thought to be a relative placement. It was not a relative placement and no approval for placement was given to CPS or the Juvenile Court. Had the children been harmed in any way, CPS would have earned another headline in the newspaper. The family relationship needed verification through birth certificates or the family needed to be licensed as a foster home.

Failure to provide similar protection for children that is expected of parents is all too common with CPS. Violations and malfeasance are swept behind a veil of secrecy or blamed on Social Worker error. CPS would not believe the parents had progressed in counseling to be ready for reunification; yet, they believed that the parents were related to the family with whom the children would live. For the children the parents actually made the right decision. The children were placed with fellow church members. In spite of the regular court reviews, neither the judge, the attorneys, nor review committees picked up on this potentially harmful violation of fundamental CPS policy.

Various checks and balances are in place to avoid these problems and to assure full compliance with CPS policy:

1. A supervisor had to sign-off on the out-of-state placement and to release money for transportation and related expenses. It is questionable that the Juvenile Court authorized medical treatment for the children. No mechanism was in place to pay for those services unless the families worked out some arrangement.

2. The receiving state had no legal authority over the children or the family taking care of the children.

3. An attorney was appointed to represent the children in Juvenile Court. The young man did not know the name of his attorney. If the attorney was paid by the county to represent the children, he should have felt an obligation to talk with them periodically. I would expect this attorney would have felt his obligation was to make decisions based on what he believed was in the children's best interest. As teenagers their

desires should have been presented to the judge and let him make the final decision. Even if the judge had ruled against the children's wishes, an appeal should have been filed and the children brought back to testify. In either case the attorney did a great disservice to the children. He allowed CPS to place the children without requiring formal proof the placement was appropriate for the children.

4. The Attorney-General represents state CPS before the Juvenile Court and was remiss in verifying the placement was approved through the ICPC and the evidence presented to the judge was accurate. The AG needed to see verification of the blood relationship between the two families or a completed home study supporting the worthiness of the family to care for the children.

5. The judge should have reviewed copies of a home study as well as the birth certificates verifying relative placement. He also should have required assurance from the children's attorney that they fully understood the direction of the case, the anticipated

length of separation from their parents and an assurance they accepted the placement. At each six month Review Hearing, a judge should require each dependent minor under review should appear in court. As part of that appearance the judge should talk to the minors with their attorney in chambers.

6. There were a number of "red flags" that someone should have recognized and questioned. All the checks and balances failed. In this case there was a Review Board meeting periodically to monitor the case. Although these were lay people, they should have been better trained. When a child is declared a Ward of the Juvenile Court, each person accepts responsibility of the child that is no different than the responsibility toward a family member. Unless people are willing to do this, they should rethink their involvement. Although checks and balances are set up to protect children, they don't work if people and professionals treat these children as an 8-5 job. The system did little right to protect these children

Neither of these children will ever request assistance from any Social Service agency.

# CHAPTER THREE

# CHECKS AND BALANCES

Since the early days of CPS children have periodically been lost or harmed while in the legal care, custody and control of Child Protective Services. No information exists as to totals of children in the various headings of: misplaced, injured, suicide or killed. It is still another example of the secrecy and lack of accountability that protects CPS. Lawsuits are settled out-of-court with restrictions against discussing the case. How many cases involve a parent absconding with his child? Did the parent believe he had no recourse and the deck was stacked against him? How many children have run from foster care? Why does the child do this? If CPS is to improve, shouldn't these children and parents be asked these questions?

The problem for foster parents is similar to biological parents. We train foster parents in how to deal with special needs children, but no training is given to care providers on understanding themselves and their reaction to stress in their lives. When foster parents come across a child who instinctively knows how to push the wrong buttons and who is secretively and persistently destructive of the foster parent's home, prized possessions and ego, frustration will build inside until an incident triggers an explosion. Similarly to the biological parent the foster parent gets caught up and drawn into the child's world rather than drawing the child into the more sophisticated world of the adult. Although regret immediately sets in, it is too late.

As newspapers publish accounts of these incidences, CPS responds to harsh criticism by offering various checks and balances to their cases. Over the years the Juvenile Court became concerned and initiated its own system.

Volunteer lay people act as a Guardian ad Litem or a Court Appointed Special Advocate, who investigate services provided in the cases, observe visits, meet with various professionals involved with the case and make recommendations to the court. Their reports and recommendations are submitted to the court. These volunteers are supervised by a salaried administrator connected to the court.

In an effort to prevent foster children from getting lost or languishing in the system, many CPS jurisdictions have gone to some sort of review system to make independent reports to the court. These review boards or committees consist of volunteer lay people also. The review boards might meet a few weeks before the six month Court Hearing. The Case Manager is obligated to be there but not the attorneys. Relatives, parents and other interested parties are invited to the meeting.

The panel is supervised by a salaried supervisor of the Superior Court. As with the Guardian ad Litem, the review boards do not have the credentials to testify in court but the judge does recognize the reports and admits them into evidence. The reports do not have any teeth to move the court in a certain direction and are usually supportive of CPS. It is disconcerting that the attorneys do not participate in these meetings. As retired citizens most of these board members have no experience in understanding related or alternative programs that might be used to achieve reunification. No supervisor will chance losing his job to encourage any challenge of the CPS position or authorize a report critical of CPS. One person from the review board should be selected to visit the parent in his living room, ask questions and observe decorations in the home. Unless this is done no emotional consideration is given the family. Their recommendations are based on a preconceived opinion garnered from the Worker's report. They are no different from the psychologist.

The board member should take the child out for a treat and listen to his feelings toward his parent. The board might observe a visit between parent and child. It is also important to visit with the child periodically as a check on the foster home. All this is time-consuming but very worthwhile. A more balanced view of the family has to be actively sought out before blindly accepting CPS recommendations. Even if the home visits support the CPS view, the board will have done a thorough job and will have met its responsibility to fully evaluate the case plan and to make an independent judgment. Look to the child to direct your decisions.

We should never believe everything we read or hear. The same holds true in accepting someone's assessment without an independent investigation. We must avoid any hint of the deck being stacked against reunification when it cannot be supported by clear and convincing evidence. As brought up earlier, a parent will not fight so hard to have his child returned unless there is a strong love and bond between parent and child. CPS should encourage people questioning their assessment. A Worker who challenges the CPS directed case plan will not last long in his employment with CPS and he will not advance in his employment either. Just as in appointing two investigators to a case, child welfare families and children will be assured justice for each child in foster care by CPS having its case plan stand up to objective scrutiny by an outside agency not having any ties to CPS.

# CHAPTER FOUR

# PARENTS AND STEP-PARENTS

One of the most difficult jobs in the world might be as a step-father to teenagers. Step-mothers are able to give nurturance, love and bake cookies. They have an innate ability to effectively handle each situation that might arise in a "blended" family. Step-fathers need a support group to avoid all the land mines in their path and men will surely step in them. When children beat up on their mother, the mother will take it all in very calmly, bake cookies and everything is back to normal and forgotten. The step-father sees what is happening to his wife and the 'Mars' in him wants to jump in and save her. A step-father needs to step back and leave all the parenting to his wife. Mixed messages need to be avoided at all cost. A step-father should try for a harmonious relationship with his step-children and count his blessings if he achieves it. Angry teenagers do not think through the repercussions before retaliating against their step-father.

A step-father is less likely to have a bond with his step-child that stops him from stepping over the line. Without that bond a step-father might lose control and do serious harm to a child. Many children have a natural resentment that their father is not in the home. They may blame their mother or even their father, but they are not willing to turn over their father's role to an intruder. If at all possible a mother should place her infant with an approved babysitter rather than with a step-father who has not demonstrated patience in handling all the demands of an infant. One child was severely abused by his mother's boyfriend because the infant would not stop crying during a football game on TV. It just takes an instant.

Middle schools have a golden opportunity to work with young boys and girls to teach about the important roles of fathers and mothers and the importance of preserving those friendships beyond divorce. A father should be willing to get up in the middle of the night to tend to his crying child. Fathers are now recognizing the need to use this time to bond with their child. More fathers than ever before are stepping up to be full-time parents to their children, when the mother is not willing or able. Fathers are appearing at Juvenile Court to claim their child when the mother has lost custody of her child. Fathers are viewed skeptically as a qualified parent; consequently, they have to jump through time delaying hoops to prove they are capable. Even mothers with severe drug problems can successfully prevent the father from acquiring his child. The father is not given equal rights by the court as the mother is. The court joins CPS in approving counseling because the father has not been active in his child's life for a significant period of time. If the mother gets custody and finds someone to replace the father, she can subtly deny contact between father and child. As the father sees his child support checks

47

used for other purposes than for his child, he may stop making payments. It has long been understood that the longer a child remains in foster care, the more distant he grows from his family. It is similar to a "V", with the parent and child growing away from the center. It is similar for non-custodial parents. The more one parent makes it difficult for the other parent to see the child, the less likely the non-custodial parent stays to fight through it. It does not mean that the bond falls apart, however. If that child is in foster care, CPS spends an inordinate amount of time reintroducing a child to his father and making certain he and his child have bonding and attachment counseling. In the case of the duct taped child, the judge wanted to delay immediate reunification because he felt the child had bonded with the foster family. This is nonsense, as a child does not readily transfer a bond beyond the age of three.

As suggested earlier, middle schools should support teaching young boys and girls to work through differences in divorces or breakup of relationships in order to maintain a strong bond with the non-custodial parent. Parents need to put differences aside and remain friends. This has become a forgotten need of children. There is no reason that a parent's return to the child should not be viewed as good for the child. If a parent should appear in the Juvenile Court after the child is removed from the custodial parent and request custody of his child, the Juvenile Court should stipulate the non-custodial parent is deemed to be capable of parenting the child and order placement with extended family of the non-custodial parent with unsupervised visits at the home of the relative. The quicker the child is returned to his parent the better. The judge needs to take the lead and meet with the non-custodial parent or both parents and child in chambers. The child will lead him to make the right decision.

# CHAPTER FIVE

# DRUG ADDICTED PARENTS

When it comes to predicting cases destined for severance, drugs are in first place in carrying drug addicted parents down a relentless path to severance and adoption. Unless the medical profession can find a way to control the addict's craving for his drug of choice, children in out-of-home placement will continue to increase. Drugs do not necessarily make parents abusive or neglectful, but the abuse of drugs does. When the craving and use of drugs jeopardizes rent payments, desire to keep a house clean, put food on the table, or provide adequately for a child's positive growth and development, a Dependency Petition needs to be filed. Drugs are insidious because of the constant craving to experience the first high again and again. It is a relentless driving force that makes people powerless to control. One professional reported he had a daily fight against resumption of drug usage. Every time he saw something white it elicited a compunction to use cocaine. Drugs are also becoming more and more potent.

During my nine years on the reservation, I was deeply saddened to have to remove children from their home. Efforts to help parents maintain sobriety were not successful for the most part. One mother stopped me on the street and asked to have her children removed because she was using her welfare and food stamps on drugs. One mother would inject fluid into her arms to make it look like she had a disability. Then she would make the rounds of churches and charities with her children to solicit money. These were fine and decent people who would use drugs again if given a fresh drug free start to life. Most will lose their children and their lives before their forty-second birthday. By keeping the children close to their parent, the ability of the children to resist the same temptations as their mother was substantially increased but not totally eradicated.

CPS and the Juvenile Court are conflicted in finding a solution to developing a case plan. Currently many jurisdictions are requiring Case Managers develop two case plans - one for reunification and one for severance of parental rights. One school of thought is that each family should be offered services to achieve reunification. The other is diametrically opposed to reunification and is punitive. This group believes children do not need to languish in foster care when the chances of the parent maintaining sobriety can never be assured. These children should have permanency in their lives. Historically these cases are impossible to move quickly through the Juvenile Court process. Without strong evidence substantiating severance, drug addicted parents can run a game which stalls the case until the children outgrow the window of opportunity for successful adoption. Drug addiction alone does not and should not constitute evidence for severance, neither should it deprive contact between parent and child.

A punitive approach does not satisfy the concern for the mental health of the child. Children are bonded to their parent and suffer life-changing trauma from their removal and attempts to place them in a permanent setting. There are always exceptions to the rule, but no research has been done to substantiate either course of action. The removal of these children is comparable to the removal of Native American children from their family. As adults we look for logic in solving the problem but logic is not understood by young children. Even adoption of a child over the age of three cannot be advocated. So much of a child's success in life is predicated on genetics. Research and experience indicate a correlation between drug use by both parents and a child's ability to reach his full potential. A myriad number of side effects from drug abusing parents cause a problem in the child's motor development, intellectual processes, Attention Deficit Disorder and susceptibility to an early onset of drug experimentation and addiction than other children. I know of no greater reason to avoid drugs during child bearing years than having to watch a new-born infant withdraw from the drugs the mother took during her pregnancy. Even the biological father's drug usage has an impact on his child.

Based on the extent of drug usage, CPS should not be required to provide the services needed to maintain sobriety in the parent. The judicially imposed requirements that CPS demonstrate efforts to reunify in order to receive federal funding should be waived. The continued efforts to achieve reunification beyond appropriate time limits does a disservice to the child. The answer to this dilemma must rest in the availability of extended family to step in and provide the stable placement the child needs. Efforts to place a child with extended family needs to be pursued with the filing of the Dependency Petition. Formal licensing requirements should be held in abeyance and allow the Worker in consort with the parent to place the child with an extended family member. The foster care payment would be used to offset the added expenses to the family. The Worker and the parent should be entrusted to make this decision as a team. The case would then be transferred to a Long-Term

Foster Care Unit, which would focus all its attention on the child's medical and educational needs. All reunification efforts would be postponed until the parent provides substantial proof of sobriety over a prolonged period of time. The Worker should not be required to hunt up the parent for proof of sobriety, income and housing. The focus on the child is not to deprive the parent of contact with his child but to place the responsibility of drug treatment directly on the parent rather than state CPS. In Illinois, prisons were built but funding problems interfered with their use. Some communities have begun efforts to open them as treatment centers for addicts. Juvenile Court judges might court order the parent to complete this type of program.

So much of CPS focus is on qualifying for federal financial incentives received for placing children in foster care to placement in a permanent home. This focus eliminates creative thinking and experimentation of new ideas. Placement with extended family should be the first course of action for any case but is often curtailed by expectations the parent will jeopardize the success of that placement in some way detrimental to the child. This casts the family as unable to protect the child. It fails to realize the strength of the family to bring about change and redirect parents and children toward success. The family is the only unit qualified to do this. They just need the support and counsel of child welfare agencies, the Juvenile Court and schools to accomplish these goals. Families need to be considered as a resource in protecting children at risk.

# CHAPTER SIX

# FINANCIALLY STRESSED FAMILIES

CPS receives federal funding for placing children in foster care. With financially stressed families the decision to file a Dependency Petition jeopardizes the chance for reunification. This applies to the 30% category of cases. If 600,000 children are in out-of-home placement the 30% adds up to unnecessary pressures on Workers and eventual burn-out. In cases where appropriate, the children might be placed temporarily with relatives until appropriate services can be lined up to work with the family intact. This avoids transferring the family's welfare payments (AFDC), to CPS coffers. The welfare payments would continue for the family provided the children are placed with relatives and returned by the end of the month. This problem is never understood or given the proper consideration by CPS investigators or Ongoing Workers. It is impossible for these financially stressed families to keep housing should their children be removed. Once public housing is taken away from a family it could take a year for housing to be available again as too many applications for housing stand in the way. Even welfare cannot be restarted until the parent has custody of the children.

Parents receiving financial assistance usually do not have the job skills to secure employment. When a CPS investigator decides to remove a child from a welfare parent, he is oblivious to the domino effect of his actions. It is the punitive mind-set of CPS that looks to find guilt rather than taking the time to accurately assess the situation. When removal is in that gray area, sensitivity must be given to the family's loss of income, housing and independence. Normal families may have a child removed but the parent still has his job. Loss of financial assistance from Aid to Families with Dependent Children (AFDC), Food Stamps, or Social Security Disability (SSI) will cause the family to lose any chance for reunification.

# CHAPTER SEVEN

# THE JUVENILE COURT PROCESS

The Juvenile Court is connected to the Superior Court, but it does not have the same Rule of Law, and acceptance of its court orders. Highly qualified attorneys refuse to practice in the Juvenile Court because "it has its own laws". Of course the drop in pay a Superior Court attorney would have to accept in representing clients in Juvenile Court is substantial. Although the Juvenile Court deals with child welfare cases and juvenile delinquents, it lacks trial by jury. More and more youth are being tried as adults which underlines the problem of the Juvenile Court not having the same authority as the Superior Court. The victims of crimes would not accept a teenage perpetrator of a vicious crime to be tried in a court lacking a Rule of Law as well as not having a trial by jury. Another significant problem is juveniles are released at the age of eighteen. Essentially the Juvenile Court turns young people loose even though they may not be ready to be released and trusts future offenses will be handled by the Superior Court. Parents are not prosecuted by the Juvenile Court. These cases are remanded to the Superior Court for prosecution. If found guilty and incarcerated for a long enough time to deprive a child parental emotional and physical support, the parent might be brought to the Juvenile Court to relinquish his parental rights or face severance based on the deprivartion issue..

Times are changing and the Juvenile Court needs to change with it or become outmoded. The increase in drug usage by parents, the disappearance of parents responsible for child support, the teen committing violent crimes, divorces involving domestic violence, and child abuse require the Juvenile Court be granted the authority to try these cases, because they all involve family and child welfare. These cases do not need to languish in the Juvenile Court until submitted to the Superior Court level. By instituting jury trials and incorporating measures to establish a Rule of Law, the Juvenile Court might be considered a separate entity with full power and authority to handle divorce, child custody, child welfare, and guardianship cases, and all crimes committed by juveniles. These cases would be handled more expeditiously by the Juvenile Court.

Certainly the Juvenile Court venue is more appropriate to try cases having previous referrals to the Juvenile Court or originally opened in the Juvenile Court. The Juvenile Court orders would need to be recognized by other jurisdictions. By improving the Juvenile Court, the Superior Courts would bring their calendars some relief. Quality attorneys would now be willing to practice in the Juvenile Court because the pay provided them through the modified court would make it worthwhile. The attorneys now practicing in the Juvenile Court would need to improve to compete with the better attorneys. The new Juvenile Court would no longer function at a lower standard. By shifting from subjective to objective standards, families and children will benefit. It will force CPS to be more selective in filing Dependency Petitions. The agency will find a higher standard will not allow them to continue manipulating the court and families. Many AG's do not relish court trials and avoid them whenever possible.

Several years ago the Missouri state police picked up a mother and two children on the interstate for a traffic infraction. She was found to be drug addicted and her children were placed in foster care until placed with the father under the Interstate Compact for the Placement of Children. After a period of monitoring the children's placement with the father, the Missouri Juvenile Court awarded complete care, custody and contol of the children with their father. The mother moved to a state out west, obtained an attorney and he filed a petition on the mother's behalf to force the father to return the children to the mother. She was able to do this without having to prove she had custody of the children. When the police showed up at the father's doorstep, the police would not recognize the

Missouri custody order. The case went all the way up to the governor's office. After much haggling between the two states, the children were allowed to remain with the father. It was a lesson on how a court can be victimized. The Missouri Juvenile Court did not have the authority to sever the mother's rights and/or place legal care, custody and control with the father. Juvenile Courts across the country need to be granted full faith and credit in court orders.

Even a cursory review of the 30% of cases under discussion in this book would reveal most parents do not give up on the runification process. One would think a parent would be relieved that CPS has taken such an incorrigible child away; yet, these same parents are still in court a year later for yet another court review of their case. They will not give up and go away as CPS might wish. One of my first introductions to CPS was a family traveling through town. They left their teen son at our CPS office and continued on their way. Fortunately these families are in the minority. The perception foisted on the general public that most child abuse cases are similar to this family is not based in reality. The Juvenile Court process separates itself from a hands-on approach, thereby, falling lock-step in line with CPS recommendations. The one avenue to glimpse a favorable family view is the CASA or Guardian ad Litem program, but these lay volunteers must have the discretion to criticize the CPS services or recommendations.

Around 30% of families are referred to CPS as a result of a one-time occurrence of stress and crisis in their lives. These families usually have been following a path leading to the referral for some time but didn't realize things were about to explode. They become frustrated and act without thinking things through correctly. Again middle schools would be the ideal time to teach young people about resources to help handle adult and family crises. Too often young couples do not find resolution to their problems quickly enough. They do not know where to go for assistance with unemployment insurance, job training, day care, infant formulae, and many other problems. In these courses young people could learn how unemployment insurance is determined and how a person qualifies for it.

My perspective garnered from working with these types of cases is the parent loves his child but is willing to give in to the Dependency Petition to avoid a pulling match with CPS, and his son in the middle. Parents also want to spare their son from testifying in court. What the parent does not realize initially is the deck is stacked against him. No judge will risk his career going up in smoke because he denied a CPS request to remove, only to have the child abused in the home. This also applies to each "professional" involved in the case. If the judge were to observe the interaction of parent and child in chambers, he would certainly be more critical of the child remaining in foster care for an inordinate period of time. But judges, attorneys and all the professionals related to the case isolate themselves from any emotional tie to families. They are afraid of letting empathy into the judicial process but they must if they want to curtail running rough-shod over less sophisticated families. It is gut-wrenching to pull a three year old child from a visit with his/her parent to return to the foster home, especially if the original allegation is not so serious that it couldn't be resolved by leaving the child in the home with services.

Of greater concern is the length of time the child remains separated from his parent. The parental nurturing and the daily interactions among family members cannot be filed away in a child's memory bank to be brought back later in life. The young girl who spent two years in foster care and missed out on her brother's birth is treated so cavalierly by these professionals. Whether good or bad memories, we need to use these memories to formulate our lives. The length of placement out of the home is rarely challenged by attorneys. The judge and the entire Juvenile Court process appear to rubber stamp CPS recommendations.

A few factual stories offer an insight to the dilemma facing CPS and parents. A teenager and his father frequently rode on cross country bicycle excursions together. The father was a supervisor in a hospital cafeteria. One day the father and son were riding together through town when they inexplicably got into a fight. Police phoned CPS and the investigator placed the child in a foster home and filed a Dependency Petition with the Juvenile Court. The father was not tried for child abuse nor did he serve any time in jail. Because of income the father was not appointed an attorney. This needs to be changed. Each parent should be appointed an attorney at county's expense, because most judges do not want parents representing themselves. Attorneys draw a judge's attention and respect, a parent representing himself does not.

This father did not fight CPS. His position was that if CPS could control his son better than he, they were welcome to try. This is another case where CPS failed to investigate the referral thoroughly or admit later they had made a mistake in removing the young man. The father attempted numerous times to get his son to achieve passing grades in high school, stop hanging with the wrong friends and stop smoking marijuana. The young man remained a Ward of the Court and remained in custody of CPS until he turned eighteen. He also continued to smoke marijuana, ditch school and associate with like-minded friends. The father's power and authority had been irretrievably usurped by CPS. The cost of foster care, medical coverage, school supplies, clothing, salaries of all the professionals involved was an unnecessary burden placed on taxpayers. All the professionals could not influence the young man to change his behavior. The adversarial and punitive approach of CPS failed to elicit the father's help in determining the best treatment for the young man.

The second story also involves a call from police that a mother had reported her husband and father of her son had struck their son sending the child into the couch. Unlike other investigations this one began with talking to the father, who reported that his fourth grade son was already getting into gangs, doing poorly in school and challenging the father's authority at home. He wanted his son to accomplish more in life than he did, which was driving a cement truck. As I took the boy outside I noticed he had a blue bandana hanging from his back pocket, used to identify affiliation with the "Crips" gang.

Another way of identifying a Crips member was in their homework assignments or notes passed in class. Each letter "B" would be crossed out because it represented the "B" in the "Bloods" gang. At one time the local elementary school principal had shown me a drawer full of red and blue bandanas he had taken from students. The principal also shared that when he asked parents to come to school and discuss the problem, the parents themselves were wearing a bandana.

I informed the child that neither his father nor I would allow him to fail and the consequences to continued gang involvement would not be to his liking. I also gave my support to the father that he was right to be concerned with his son, but there were services to address the problem. I suggested services I could provide to assist him, either in counseling for his son or changing schools. I did not force any treatment on him but left it up to him to contact me if he needed help.

All Dependency Petitions are processed through the Juvenile Court. The Juvenile Court Judge sets a hearing date for the parents but the child does not appear in court. The judge declares the child a Ward of the Court and assigns legal care, custody and control of the child to CPS. The judge also routinely places an "efforts statement" in the Court Order that CPS has made every effort to avoid removing the child. This statement is necessary for CPS to receive financial remuneration from the Federal Government. Research would show judges routinely provide CPS this statement, but they do not routinely perform a critical analysis of the efficacy of services provided by CPS. They sit on the bench, listen to the arguments and rubber stamp CPS recommendations. Opening files will show some collusion of the courts, attorneys and CPS. No attorney has ever challenged the "efforts statement". Parents are not sophisticated enough to realize their attorney may not be providing adequate representation if no challenge is made. A parent should not have faith in an attorney who serves two masters.

Until the case is dismissed, the Juvenile Judge assumes full responsibility for the child's well-being; yet, the judge rarely sees or talks to the child. If anything ever happens to the child, the judge and attorneys are protected by CPS. The media will report on injury and death to foster children, but neither judges nor attorneys are ever questioned. Instead the media track down CPS which cites confidentiality or Worker error in maintaining secrecy. The media lamely accept the ruse rather than using its investigative skills to locate the parent or other relatives who might shed some knowledge on the matter. In September of 2003 a toddler died in foster care. A hospital staff member was implicated in the death because she did not notice or report what should have been recognized as abuse. Lawsuits are settled out of court with a gag order attached. Files on these cases need to be opened and researched to determine the appropriateness of the case plan. Focus was put on the hospital staff member rather than investigating CPS activity in monitoring the child in placement. Elected officials periodically call for sweeping changes in child welfare systems but changes never seem to occur unless it is to add more paperwork for the Social Workers. If checks and balances were working properly the death of this child should never have happened.

Protecting a foster child from harm is not difficult if each professional is doing his job properly. CPS over the past several years has been shifting responsibilities of the Worker away from a personal involvement with the case through requiring completion of expanding paperwork, increased caseloads, plus so many reports, meetings and court appearances that the Worker cannot possibly keep up with the necessary client contacts he is responsible to maintain. If CPS were to give a Worker a choice between finishing a paperwork responsibility and making a visit with the child, do you think CPS would excuse him from the paperwork? The Worker should not have to decide between spending time on relentless paperwork and visiting a foster child. CPS mistakenly requires both. When an atrocity occurs, the Worker should be allowed to give his account of what happened. Instead these Workers disappear from sight after the media publishes the story. It smacks of making a deal to not file charges against the Worker in exchange for his remaining quiet.

Of further concern is the reocurring transfer of cases from Worker to Worker and judge to judge. Whenever a parent moves his case has to be transferred to the office handling that geographical area. With judges the case is reassigned to fit in an opening in a judge's calendar around the next six month hearing. When a Worker is assigned a new case, he would have to read it at home to fully understand the history. In an effort to maintain contact with foster children, CPS administrators contract out various minor responsibilities of Workers to free them up to stay on top of their work. Instead of the Worker taking foster children to visits with families, another agency is paid to do this as well as do drug drops, transportation to counseling appointments, and related services for which the Worker does not have time. More money is taken from taxpayers to pay others to do the Case Manager's job. A side goal is to diffuse responsibility for those ever-present negative news articles. CPS will suggest the contracting for related services allows more contact with the foster children. This sounds good but all these "professionals" work 8-5 jobs. The love, nurturance and guidance a foster child receives must be provided by the foster family. The child invariably loses an understanding of his Worker's role in his life and loses trust in his Worker. The Worker becomes a stranger to the child, but more importantly the Worker drifts from an emotional involvement with the child. It is no wonder the child might resent being abandoned by everyone in his life. Many begin to act out in foster care because these are the only people at whom he can express his anger. It is no different for extended family. If regular contact with nephews and nieces is not ensured, the relationship is weakened. An extended family member cannot save a niece or nephew from failure if the child has not been repeatedly exposed to the genuine love and concern of that family member. Extended family members must spend time listening to and encouraging their nephew or niece to share his/her most personal, private and intimate problems.

Too frequently attorneys never meet with the child they represent in Juvenile Court. Many times I found a child could not name his attorney. The salary the child's attorney receives can be likened to a welfare check for the attorney. These attorneys need to provide a critical analysis of CPS recommendations, but they do not want to risk losing that check. If they accept the salary, they should want to do the job. The lack of adequate representation by attorneys for children is one of the scams in the Juvenile Court process and needs to be investigated. Children have no one else to fight for them and denying a child fulfillment in his wish to return to his family is a great disservice to children. If court transcripts are researched, no mention of the child's wishes will be found to emanate from the child's attorney.

The Juvenile Court Judge must provide a leadership role in requiring that each Worker and/or attorney is doing his job properly. The judge and Worker's supervisor must verify contacts with the child. The child's attorney should have to submit evidence to the judge he has had personal contact with each child he represents. Too many frivolous cases prevent Workers and attorneys from doing a credible job in protecting children. For CPS the more cases brought into the Juvenile Court the more money received from the Federal Government, the greater the need for hiring more workers and so on. In time the Worker suffers burn out. Good Workers move on to other jobs.

The Juvenile Court judge must institute periodic meetings with CPS administrators to focus on more thorough investigation to avoid filing specious cases and more quickly achieving reunification of children with their biological family. The judge might refuse to issue the "efforts statement", if reunification is not achieved more quickly. The Juvenile Court must resist being a rubber stamp for CPS.

The Juvenile Court transfers legal care, custody and control from the parent to CPS, but the child remains a Ward of the Court. As such the judge is responsible for that child. The judge sets a case review and appoints attorneys to represent the parent and dependent minors at future hearings. The attorneys are paid with county funds. Because the pay does not approach that of attorneys at the Superior Court level, attorneys are unwilling to jeopardize their careers in advocating for child welfare clients. If the attorney is too aggressive in challenging CPS, new cases may not be assigned to him or he will not be offered a contract the next year. In other words a "team player" will be assured of continuing to receive cases. His dreams and goals of success in private practice or jury trials will remain alive. His success represents an important stepping stone toward becoming an Attorney-General or a Juvenile Court pro-tempore judge. The quality of representation can be demonstrated by the attorney who told his client to just do whatever CPS wanted. This was an attorney who meekly accepted the status quo rather than attempting to adequately defend his client at any cost. Attorneys like this have no business in the Juvenile Court. Attorneys get an easy paycheck for just showing up and going through these motions. Pay schedules should be revised to more adequately compensate attorneys and bring other attorneys into the Juvenile Court.

When a foster child comes under media attention, newspaper reporters should demand answers from the Juvenile Court judge. The judge has to be held responsible for each child in his ward-ship. If a child is a Ward of the Juvenile Court, that child should be expected to appear at each court review and meet with his attorney and the judge in chambers. In this way the judge will ascertain the child's needs are being met, and the child's attorney is representing him properly. The judge will also have an opportunity to determine the availability of extended family to care for the minor and give the child the chance to express his wishes directly to the judge. If these measures are not adopted, lawsuits should be brought against the entire judicial system. No one should settle out of court with a gag order keeping the facts of the case hidden from the media and the public. Unless CPS is willing to open their files, these cases will continue to be hidden from public scrutiny and children will continue to be deprived of reunification.

An example was an allegation of sexual molest by a mother's boyfriend which was later thrown out by a higher court for insufficient evidence. That same allegation continued to be treated as fact by the CPS Worker and the reports to Juvenile Court characterized the mother as 'in denial'; thus, she was considered to be unable to adequately protect her child. Eventually the mother was persuaded to agree to an "open adoption" arrangement. Unfortunately open adoption is not enforceable in court. Visits continued for mother and child at a neutral site until the adoption was finalized. It was heart-rending when the child asked his mother when he would return home. We can point to the obvious improvement for the child in a better home with two parents, but does the child agree with that assessment or does he really need it? The Indian Child Welfare Act requires the judge to question parents relinquishing their parental rights as to their understanding of their actions. The judge might also ask if adoption were not successful what they would prefer for their child's placement. If their suggestion would be to place the child with a member of the extended family, then we have a parent having second thoughts about adoption.

The point is many of these adoptions are pushed on the parents surreptitiously and without considering an alternative placement with extended family. The judge trusts CPS to handle the case, but he never looks into how severance and adoption were handled. Over time the Worker pressures the parent into submission. It is not the court that decides against the mother's parental rights to her child, but the CPS administration. The judge's blind acceptance of the recommendations makes him complicit in the subterfuge. Certainly this child would never have agreed with the adoption if he could have had a say. At the age of five he is not allowed to question the adoption. As it is he has to feel his mother shunned him but he still loves her. Since the judge was operating from his ivory tower, it was relatively easy to make the decision.

The question still remains whether adoption was formulated through coercion or dismissal of relative placement without giving relative placement an honest trial.

The judge should have met with the mother, child and attorneys in chambers before agreeing to the adoption. The child's relatives might also have been present to sign a form refusing to care for the child. There is no doubt the parent had problems caring for her child, but these were medical not abusive problems. Even foster care until the child reached an age to help in his own care would have been preferable.

There is no doubt the adopting couple would provide a stable and loving home for the child. The question comes down to our right to expect a child to transfer his parental bond from his biological mother to another. We are becoming too cavalier in these matters. Getting the case dismissed in court becomes the objective rather than preserving families. It is up to the court to review these relinquishment cases to insure the correct decision was made. This cannot be done unless the judge meets with the parent and child in chambers or open court with a relative also present to give consent.

By rubber stamping CPS recommendations in Court Reports, the Chief Judge of the Juvenile Court permits the miscarriage of justice to families and children. By appointing pro-tempore judges from the ranks of attorneys not capable of practicing in higher courts, the Chief Judge fails to raise the standards of his court, and he continues the expectation of rewarding "team players" over independent and aggressive pursuit of justice. If the Chief Judge were to step in with formal orders that he knows are needed for CPS to do their job properly, he could set a different tone to ensure just and fair treatment of families. Chief Judges are obligated to serve one year in Juvenile Court and return to Superior Court. One year is not enough time to make significant changes. Currently families able to afford their own private attorney achieve reunification much more quickly than those required to accept court-appointed attorneys.

# CHAPTER EIGHT

# CASE STUDIES

A single mother and her four year old son were having difficulties in their relationship. The mother sought counseling from a reputable agency. The mother and counselor felt the child was unusually oppositional and not bonded. Eventually the counselor recommended the mother consider signing relinquishment papers with the Adoption Unit of CPS. The child was placed in a foster-adoption (fost-adopt) home, a Dependency Petition was filed with the Juvenile Court, and the mother was obligated to pay a nominal fee each month until her child was formally adopted. All contact between parent and child was discontinued. Worker comments indicated there was extreme hatred of the child toward his mother. Because the child tore up all pictures of his mother, no visits with the mother were allowed.

The child proceeded to fail in one adoptive home after another. As time progressed, he was diagnosed with Attention Deficit Disorder and prescribed Ritalin. The medication seemed to help him control his behavior so much that his foster parent stated he would try removing the daily medication from the child. Shortly after, the child's behavior regressed and the medication was resumed. Adoption as a goal was eliminated and the child continued in foster homes until finally institutionalized in a boys' home in another city. The child seemed to progress so well that an adoptive home was located for him.

The child was a high school student. Eventually the adoptive parents caught him leaving at night through his bedroom window to party and drink alcohol. He would return by early morning and go to school. The (Boys'

Home) program terminated his enrollment and I brought him back. During a conversation I asked him if he would like to see his mother. He did not show much excitement but he did not dismiss the offer. Hatred toward his mother was not the opposite of love. Indifference would have concerned me more. Hatred as with love involves a strong emotion, which could swing just as quickly to love or at least acceptance.

In this case CPS failed the family in two fundamental areas. The mother had been paying a monthly fee until her son's adoption was finalized. When CPS could not achieve adoption, she should have been brought in to discuss ideas regarding the future of her son. Over the several years this became a hefty amount of money she had to pay. The second failure was not to explain the discovery of ADD and how medication was helping her son control his behavior. If the ADD had interfered with his ability to bond to her or anyone, then perhaps the medication would help in a successful reunification. CPS could have offered intensive counseling programs to assist the mother. CPS was unwilling to consider this option or worse, it probably never occurred to them. Neither the judge nor attorneys reviewing the case for so many years challenged the direction of the case plan. These are the people entrusted with protecting the best interests of children. One Worker's comment that the child tore up his mother's picture was misinterpreted as an unwillingness to see his mother. No one had asked the young man what he wanted. The young man may have been angry that his mother gave up on him, when actually the counselors were responsible for not considering a medical problem was interfering with the bonding process. There are so many similar cases needing a 72-hour psychiatric hospital evaluation to properly diagnose these cases rather than leaving the diagnosis in the hands of people not having any medical training. The mother was never relieved of paying the monthly fee. She knew her son better than any of the professionals involved with the child. The judge never did recognize the mother as such in court. No one was willing to connect the dots. The mother was not given sound advice by her counselor or CPS Workers to give up her son for adoption. She was given the best advice available at that time, but it does relate to a thesis of this book that a thorough investigation needed consultation with a psychiatrist along with the counselor. The counselor never advised the mother to do this and neither did the CPS Worker. To dismiss the mother/son relationship as not a good fit put the child on a path to an early death.

The lack of a medical diagnosis of ADD early in this child's life was a grave mistake. Why did the judge or attorneys not ask for a psychiatric evaluation before granting the relinquishment? On the reservation we were fortunate to have a child's psychiatric hospital available for the 72-hour evaluation. This needs to be made available to all CPS jurisdictions and its use promoted by the judges. These services are imperative if we are to expect a thorough investigation of CPS referrals.

On the reservation we had a family of a boy, who was in fourth grade, and he had five sisters. The children had been in state foster care some years earlier and this was probably known by the elementary school the children attended. I received a referral from the school that the young man's pants were soiled and I needed to take him home. What gradually became evident was the school believed the mother was sending her son to school that way. The mother denied this but it was not an every day occurrence. One day I received a call from the mother that her son was to be in court that morning for breaking into the gym and stealing some items. She asked me to be there. The judge granted my request for a 72-hour psychiatric hospital evaluation, where he was diagnosed with ADD. When the young man started taking his medication he told me he did not feel as angry and aggressive as he had felt before taking the medication. At a follow-up court hearing the judge authorized a group home placement to other alternatives for the crime he had committed. The young man was eager to go. His sisters were also eager for him to go. When I arrived at his home to take him to the group home, his sisters had his bags packed for him. Unlike the earlier story this young man was able to have the ADD diagnosed early enough to learn how to deal with the disorder and continue living with his family, even with his five sisters. The last time I saw him he gave me a thumb's up.

Attention Deficit is not easily recognized in children. It comes on so subtly that a parent or teacher might think the child is consciously misbehaving. One of the observations of the child for possible ADD is whether he/she can watch a show through from beginning to end or at least 30 minutes of it. In many of the cases involving domestic violence I found a correlation between a failure in middle school when ADD begins to balloon in a young man, the failure to identify it, and the subsequent emergence of domestic violence after marriage. It is also related to losing jobs. When a person with ADD becomes stressed in arguments he will lash out more quickly than most people. The need is to diagnose ADD early enough to teach the boy or girl how to more effectively lead a successful life. In working with another family it was against the father's culture to use medications to control behavior. The father did not want his son to be considered as "crazy". Interestingly girls may also have ADD but it is hidden better than boys. Girls are taught or learn to be less aggressive in their play than boys.

# CHAPTER NINE

# RECALCITRANT TEENS AND
# INDEPENDENT LIVING PROGRAMS

Hopefully this chapter will spur a discussion similar to Secretary Rumsfeld's snowflakes. Child Protective Services, law enforcement agencies and Juvenile Probation Programs are all facing similar problems dealing with recalcitrant teenagers. These agencies have been fighting these problems individually, but perhaps it is time to consider merging into a team of workers from each area to tackle the problems as a model program for intervention when young people first begin to show signs of being at risk for failing themselves, their parents and society. Social Workers and Juvenile Probation Officers are the experts to extrapolate from their caseloads the magnitude of teens and services needed during the next five to ten years. For years agencies have been crisis managing the epidemic outcropping of teen crimes. Through media reports we are bombarded with reports of teens stealing cars, running away from home, using risky drugs, joining gangs and going on killing sprees. Should these crimes be left to police or is there a way for agencies to join forces to find a way to provide intervention before minor problems escalate into violent behavior in a teenager? In most of these cases the "red flags" were evident, but serious intervention was not invoked.

A Model Community Team of police officers, probation officers, CPS Social Workers, and middle school educators might be formed to identify teens at risk and meet with the teen and his parent at regular intervals to track the teen's progress. Meetings would focus on performance and attendance in class, his dress patterns, friends, his acceptance of curfew, and whether legal infractions are continuing or not. The team along with the parent and teen understand at the first meeting good behavior and progress will dismiss the team's involvement. If the problems are not resolved, the team will refer the child to the Juvenile Court Judge. These ideas are based on the premise and backed up by experience that young people need to be taught how to remain at a distance to gang recruitment activities. Being involved with the team gives the young person an excuse when he is recruited. Secondly young people do behave when physically and emotionally removed from the gang environment. Many young people on the reservation were able to survive only by removing them from the rez. The team process puts the responsibility directly on the teen's shoulders. If he fails he will understand he failed and had been given a fair chance to succeed. Current policy is not controlling the increasing number of teens being drawn into more serious crimes. Historically the system has been much too lenient during the initial arrest for "small" crimes. The various agencies dealing with teens do not get together to brainstorm new ideas. We can and must do a better job.

Rather than accepting the status quo, we need to challenge our workers to find creative solutions.

For the teen failing to respond successfully to the intervention, the team will request the Juvenile Court Judge to designate the teen a Ward of the Court and court order the teen to a designated group home placement. The team approach would rely on the group home to provide the monitoring of the child that is needed. If the child continues to run away, the judge might pursue an incarceration for a short period of time, followed by a return to the same group home. The important aspect of this service is not to let the teen fail and to reward the parent's trust and faith in the team.

As we have seen in earlier chapters, CPS has overloaded its caseloads with an increasing number of teens who have not reunified with parents. By bringing teens into the Juvenile Court, CPS undermines the parent's authority with his child. Under these circumstances the parent throws up his hands and lets CPS handle the child. To make matters worse CPS never consults with the parent about his child's behavior as the case progresses through court. This has forced CPS to develop yet another program to hide and cover up their deficiencies in these teen cases.

With the gowing number of teens failing in foster care and the lack of adoptive homes for these troubled teens, CPS had to develop an alternative program to house teens not suited to foster care. Thus developed the Independent Living Programs; whereby, CPS will set up teens in their own apartment. The concept makes sense. A teen needs to prepare for life as an adult. More Workers are hired at taxpayers' expense to place these teens in apartments, pay their rent and utilities, help them locate employment, and teach them principles of budgeting their income to meet their expenses. By performing well the teen may sign a voluntary foster care agreement at the age of eighteen when the judge dismisses the case. CPS is still obligated to work with the young person because he/she does not have the skills to live independently. If the minor fails to cooperate with CPS, he may be dismissed from the program with unsatisfactory progress. Sounds like a tough love approach; yet, the child will not be accepted back. One might expect he will return to his parent and his family will take him back. How does CPS justify not continuing to work with the young person until he becomes an independent adult and able to function on his own?

The program becomes a dumping ground for case managers who cannot spend an inordinate amount of time trying in vain to locate appropriate housing and coordinating changes in placement with progress toward achieving a high school diploma. The case plan can be changed from graduation and reunification to employment and preparation for independent living. By hook or by crook the teen graduates from this program as a success and the case is closed by CPS. If the teen fails the case has already been closed by the court; so, CPS can sweep it under the carpet without having to account for their failure. No follow-up is required to determine the benefits of the program. If CPS does not even inform the public of the program, can it be performing to achieve what it was set up to do?

In some parts of the country programs have popped up asking for public donations to help homeless young people who are victims of abusive parents. These young people are presented as trying to get an education against enormous odds. Donations can even out the odds and help a young person complete his education. The fallacy of people running this program is they rely on the parent signing a statement the child is not welcome in the family. Whether the parent signs the form or not, the child needs to be referred to CPS to insure the teen comes under the protective custody of the Juvenile Court. If these programs are still in existence, they need to be investigated to determine whether these teens were abused or are merely runaways. The public should be given an accounting of where the money goes. Follow-up of young people in these programs needs to verify the programs are successful. What is the percentage of these young people completing high school or a GED successfully?

On the surface both of these programs have good intentions. The programs do need to open their records to the public. We have no evidence the programs have done what they were set out to accomplish. It would seem if they were successful there would be publicity put forth by both programs. It would be informative to know how much is spent on the average child. The programs should not receive any money unless their files are opened and follow-up studies are publicized.

These types of programs can be successful. Success begins with selective recruitment of young people who have demonstrated their readiness for the program by maintaining steady progress in school or toward a GED. Young people need to discuss openly their five year goals. There needs to be evidence the teens are drug free. They should be willing to work within the system rather than opposing it. This means getting to work on time and putting in a full days work.

# CHAPTER TEN

# GROUP HOMES

All delinquent teenagers follow a similar path and the fortunate ones will be referred to a group home placement. Once a child starts down the wrong path, we cannot expect he/she will voluntarily change unless he is taken out of the gang element. Gang-type involvement is a perplexing phenomenon. Percentage-wise girls are now rivaling boys for incorrigibility and group home placement. No defining moment rises to epitomize a child's quest for peer acceptance at the sake of discarding family values and the laws of society. Child Protective Services and Juvenile Probation Officers are besieged with delinquent teens who do not accept efforts by the courts and parents to move them away from the gang philosophy and control. We should maintain focus on the child and not look around for reasons why the child is the way he is. For years we have been too lenient on first time offenders. This is why I recommended in chapter nine a team of agencies to focus on the first time offenders at risk for continuing down that path of self-destruction. The gang will not let a member break away and the teen is also unwilling at first to break away. Once a child is removed from control by the gang, the probability of successfully helping the child is significantly improved.

As early as fourth grade the recruitment process begins and by high school these young people are on the fast track to school failure, drug addiction and eventual violence. The depth of involvement sneaks up on all of us. Whether destroying mailboxes, breaking into a house and smearing excrement on the walls, or doing a drive-by shooting, teens seem very astute at hiding their activity from their parents.

Young people join gangs to avoid being bullied, some are looking for acceptance, some seek independence, and most profess to find no value or future in family, school and society.

On the reservation students would leave home for school, change to gang clothes at a friend's house and change back after school. If a principal mailed a letter to the parent, the child merely intercepted it. With no communication between school and parents, the child is in charge. The longer a child goes undetected, the further down the path he goes. He falls further behind in school and drugs embolden him to actively defy parents and authority figures. By the time he may be picked up for possessing drug paraphernalia it is already too late. The child is now unwilling to change. He has been indoctrinated. If a young person is killed in gang activity, he dies a hero's death. Kids gather around his grave and push cigarettes into the ground as an offering to a fallen comrade. The indoctrination to the gang rituals and the fantasy of living on after death can be placed on the same level as a military or terrorist cult. Parents of these young people are generally oblivious of or in denial of the depth their child is involved. Even as evidence trickles in, the parent believes his child will respond to love, trust, common sense, family values and his child's innate goodness to redirect him. The father's assessment of his son is correct but the parent does not realize it is too late for his son to get off that path without some strong intervention. Once off that path the child begins to function properly.

Nothing is more devastating for a parent than awakening to the realization his child has been acquiescing on the surface but concealing his determination not to change. If the parent reacts with force as discipline, a referral to Child Protective Services is certain to follow. CPS assesses the referral as abuse of a minor by the parent, removes the child and files a Dependency Petition with the Juvenile Court. The failure of CPS to thoroughly evaluate the case and to later admit a mistake leaves CPS with a teen requiring crisis management until he leaves the program unless he is completely removed from any connection with his "friends" and referred to a group home. For these young people leniency is no longer an option, because any further infractions may require a trial as an adult and a felony conviction tied to the young person for the rest of his life.

A group home satisfies several concerns. Group homes are used for young people who may have exhausted a more conventional placement. Historically homes are remodeled to house six to eight young people at risk in less stringent placements. The ideal group home may be located in a small scale community. Besides the house parents one worker is assigned to monitor the child's progress in school. Chores are assigned as well as individual and group counseling sessions as needed. If the program is working properly the child will begin to focus on success in schoolwork and chores at the group home. His reward for good progress is a visit home under close supervision. The child must be aware that a court judge and his parents are in agreement he needs to be there. The court holds reviews of the teen's progress every six months. Although these programs cost around $2500./mo., the cost is off-set by the success of the child. It is vitally important for the family to be actively involved in the child's treatment and cooperate in their own counseling if required.

# CHAPTER ELEVEN

## SEVERANCE AND ADOPTION

With CPS the majority of cases moving expeditiously toward adoption are those in which the primary caretaker has an extensive history of failure to control drug addiction, or he faces several years of incarceration depriving a child parental support. In either case the outcome is obvious from the beginning, but CPS must await the final verdict. Once the case is ready for severance and/or adoption, it is ready for transfer to the Adoption Unit. People interested in adoption attend a group orientation session where CPS

Adoption Workers explain the process of adoption. Background checks, finger-printing checks, reference letters, autobiographies, physicals, and home studies are some of the requisites to qualifying for adoption. The majority of people interested in adoption desire to adopt an infant, but CPS needs families to consider older children who are more difficult to place. More and more CPS is contracting out to private agencies to find adoptive homes for CPS children. This is being forced on CPS because of their inability to adopt out the numerous children awaiting a permanent home. As already touched upon, CPS has brought this on themselves by not considering other options to foster care/adoption and to their fear of returning children to a potentially abusive environment. If CPS had better efforts in identifying extended family and offering financial incentives, children would not be sitting in foster care awaiting adoption. Unfortunately the outside agencies will run into the same problems CPS has. The inordinate length of time to reach the severance and adoption level moves the child out of the preferred age to adopt. Children reach an age in foster care where they start demonstrating behavior problems genetically inherited or learned from their biological family.

Much has been made of Bonding and Attachment Counseling programs, but even these would seem to be having problems in successfully reaching their goals. Most adoptive parents want to believe the child they are adopting will easily bond with them. Success depends solely on the strength of the child's bond with his biological parent. The older a child is, the less likely he is willing to transfer his bond to another. Counseling cannot overcome this allegiance. Adoptive parents cannot become frustrated or despondent if a bond does not seem to be developing within the child. Change will come incrementally - drop by drop. It comes over a day-to-day relationship by setting aside time to listen to your child. Listen to understand what he is saying and rephrase back to him so he knows you have fully understood him, his problems and his needs. The better a child is understood, the more willing and able he is to understand you. Do not initially set the bar too high. By intensive listening the child will guide you. Do not try to guide him.

If counseling is sought because of the child's unprovoked behavior problems, the counseling should start with assessing the strength of the biological bond and helping the child deal with understanding why his parent cannot keep him. If the bond is deep, the adoptive parents should on their own set up a visit with the biological parent at their house and watch and listen to the interaction between parent and child. If a strong bond exists, an open adoption may be the only way to resolve the problem. In this arrangement letters and pictures will be exchanged, with the child choosing the picture he might want to send. Visits should be arranged to approximate the child's desires. In cases such as this, CPS is able to arrange an adoption subsidy to cover the added expenses. There can be much satisfaction from helping a child achieve his potential as a result of your efforts with him individually as well as allowing him to have regular contact with his biological parent. Gradually as time passes, he will desire less contact with his parent. As he matures he will expend more time and energy in friends, school and later in dating. Whether he stops his contact with his biological parent or doesn't is immaterial. Either way you will have grown just as close to your child as a parent can and he to you.

Adoption today is handled much too cavalierly by CPS. CPS does not consider a child's wishes for adoption. It is similar to pre-arranged marriages, where neither party has control over his/her life. Most children under six have very little comprehension of what is happening to them. The child has very little involvement in the decision-making process. For the more difficult adoption cases CPS is able to provide an adoption subsidy. An adoption subsidy indicates the adoption is at risk. Opening these cases to the public will offer a fresh perspective on more creative methods of successfully achieving adoption. CPS must avoid relying on adoption subsidies to improve their reports of successful adoptions.

Drug usage by the biological parent will remain as the most significant cause of transferring cases for severance and adoption. The daily craving for the drug of choice can only be resisted by more intensive treatment programs than currently available. For the most part drug users represent your friends, co-workers and relatives. Extreme measures need to be taken by CPS and the Juvenile Court to expedite these children of long-term drug using parents into stable and long-term placements. There needs to be ongoing research to develop the best approaches to handling these cases. Without research we continue to inch our way through the dark maze.

A two year old boy was removed from his drug-addicted parents and placed in foster care. The mother voluntarily relinquished her parental rights but the father hoped to control his drug usage and reunify with his son. This was a noble effort. He was a good person and he loved his child. The craving for a drug is so strong that anything white will spring a need to use a drug. All the treasures a drug addict holds dear will eventually succumb to the need for another high that will surreptitiously destroy all the dreams and goals he has. The mother realized this and she made the only decision she could for her son's sake.

After the father's last positive test the father left the state. He and I had had discussions on the need for him to assure his son would be able to develop a bond with adoptive parents if he were not successful. In other words the father could harm his son's chances to develop a bond with adoptive parents if the father's sobriety could not be controlled. There was no good achieved in dragging his son with him. It would be better to sign relinquishment papers as the mother had done. His disappearance was understandable as he had high hopes of overcoming his addiction. By taking off as he did, he did not resolve his son's future as he should have. CPS would have been able to finalize adoption with the fost-adopt family in a short time had he relinquished his rights. By not doing this he forced CPS to go through time-consuming requirements which the court requires in building a case for severance.

It is interesting to see how CPS treats these drug involved cases. Most of the responsibilities assigned to the drug-addicted parent to accomplish reunification are arbitrary and capricious. A parent does not need employment to be an effective parent; yet, this is frequently required to demonstrate someone is capable of raising a child. The father could have received welfare assistance in the form of Aid for Financially Dependent Children/Food Stamps to provide for his child. Just being an AFDC/FS recipient opens the door to a number of programs in job training, day care, infant formulae, and low income housing. Workers needed to suggest to him the options, such as living with his mother or extended family and how to apply for low income housing. A parent cannot receive AFDC without having possession of his child. CPS and welfare programs do not have any agreement on how to arrange for welfare before the child is returned. It stands to reason a parent will need money to secure housing. Is it too much to expect welfare and CPS to accept a formal letter guaranteeing a child's return once welfare is approved? Another option may be living with a relative and receive AFDC/FS. In not suggesting these possibilities to the father, he located housing close to his former hang-outs and close to his old friends. I am not suggesting these measures would have been a cure for the father, but one must wonder if indeed CPS was not pushing the father down the wrong path. CPS withheld important information from the father and required certain things be accomplished that possibly put a greater burden on the father for which he was not ready to handle correctly.

One mother in a different case opted for prison incarceration for two years rather than receive drug treatment at a facility where drugs could be accessed easily. She had used these facilities in the past and she knew they would not work with drugs close by. Upon release from prison she maintained her sobriety by living with her teenage daughter at her mother's house. Extended family had frequent contact with the mother because she resided with her mother. Extended family proved in this case to be a vital resource in recovery. As she maintained her sobriety she was able to guide her daughter who had been getting into trouble while her mother was incarcerated. The bond between mother and child helped the daughter change her behavior to positive goals in life.

In this case we readily see the importance of letting the mother and child reside together. Older children in foster care do not establish a bond with anyone; therefore, they are not receptive to advice and counsel. Her daughter became the focus in her life as she placed her daughter's well-being above her need for drugs. The child accepted her mother's advice. We need research to locate creative ways to help families suffering through drug addiction and destroying themselves and their children needlessly.

People considering adoption should consider obtaining a state license as a fost-adopt home. If CPS has a child they believe will be free for adoption, that child could be placed in a fost-adopt home immediately, rather than the normal progression of foster home to foster home only to be transferred so late as to jeopardize bonding. If bonding does occur between the child and the fost-adopt family then adoption will be offered to the family. This also gives the family time to do a little research. Some problems are not readily noticeable in infants or very young children. One concern is whether the child's parent is heavily addicted to drugs or merely experimented with drugs. Side effects of drug usage may cause bonding problems, delays in motor coordination, education readiness, Attention Deficit Disorder, or an expected propensity to become addicted earlier in life than children not exposed to drugs through their parent's usage. Programs such as Developmental Disabilities are making great strides in reducing the permanent debilitation of children born addicted to drugs or susceptible to the ravages of the side effects. Fost-adopt parents need to know whether CPS would be willing to help should problems develop or not.

Adoption subsidies offer an incentive for adoption of special needs children and are expected to expand in need and usage in the future. The adoption subsidy payments to adoptive parents represent a viable alternative to freezing out continued contact with the biological family. In this respect an open adoption is preferable to a closed adoption but must be authorized by the courts and supported by the adoptive and biological parents. Extended family should also be able to qualify for adoption subsidy payments if a relative is placed in their home by CPS. CPS needs to consider extended family more readily as a resource in providing a permanent home for an abused child. They need to trust the extended family will protect the child from an abusive parent and also to make the correct decision in contacts between parent and child. To not make a sincere effort in locating a placement with extended family does a disservice to the child.

# CHAPTER TWELVE

## NON-COURT CASES

A major component of all CPS agencies should be an intervention in cases not having sufficient evidence to refer the family to the court, but some intervention is necessary to keep the family out of court. These are non-court cases and the program should receive separate funding from the Federal Government, because of the possible need to pay for foster care placement, which CPS would have to absorb by dipping into their limited budget. The benefit for CPS, the Juvenile Court and families is that services are provided on a voluntary basis with the goal of correcting the problems that led to the original allegation. All services normally provided to court cases would be available to these cases. Unlike court cases the parent and case manager would have the opportunity to work as a team, which involves cooperation and communication. It also leaves the family intact, although foster care might be required from time to time.

Historically CPS has not supported these families because of the cost involved and a certain disdain for families not able to resolve their own problems in a short period of time. If CPS is willing to provide services, they are usually time limited with one chance at foster care and that's it. 'Close the case and if another referral is received take the family to court'. For these families this approach is punitive and arbitrary. Unfortunately these families cannot resolve their problems in a short period of time. These families often survive on the edge. They will face a crisis and need help to resolve it. After a period of stability another crisis rears its ugly head and the family once again needs help in slaying the dragon. The approach of CPS does not allow for mitigating circumstances, thereby, pushing more cases into the court that do not need to be there as long as abuse or neglect is not present. A non-court case might involve a family on welfare and living in a trailer with difficult children, shut off notices, past due rent payments and a catastrophic illness. Despite all these problems the family picks up a big dog as a pet. Don't know why, they just do. If an administrator is tied to his desk, it is hard for him to develop empathy for the family. As a Worker in the middle of the battle it is different. These cases should not be managed from the top but down at the Worker's level.

An example of a case that should have been a non-court case follows:

## A CASE STUDY

The town of Guadalupe is located on the southern edge of Phoenix, AZ. along the interstate. It is comprised of Native American families. There are many problems in this community. Gangs revolve around which side of the street a family lives. In the morning men gather at a street corner ostensibly waiting to be offered a day labor job. In truth they are waiting for drugs to be dropped off. Although a major shopping center exists in walking distance, it is not considered a source of employment by most of the young people. Except for a few outreach programs set up to provide social services to the residents, the Native American community is pretty much neglected.

One family lived on an undeveloped lot close to the center of town. The lot was given to the family by a kind friend. There was no sewer connection. The sewer stopped at their driveway entrance and started again on the other side. The family had slapped discarded wood paneling together as the only protection against the elements. Water was obtained by running a garden hose to the neighbor's house. Furniture was whatever they could pick up in the community. Heat was provided by blankets and a fire. The family still used an outhouse.

Three generations of family lived here. The elderly and sickly grandparents had a long history of alcohol usage, but they were patiently waiting out their years with a toughness not seen anymore and a simple acceptance of life as a Native American. The mother was in her mid-thirties. She had two high school age boys who had dropped out of school. One of the boys was already emaciated from sniffing paint. The local fire department had had responded so many times to provide emergency treatment related to the effects of huffing that they were resigned to his eventual death. On one occasion the young man was so sick from sniffing paint that he could not get out of bed, but his friends brought cans of paint to him. Her other son had been in a boys' choral group in Phoenix and had traveled around the country performing with the group. He too had dropped out of school, but he was more into gang activity than substance abuse. He was a personable and handsome young man. The two older girls were still in school but beginning to spend just as much time in Juvenile Detention for minor shop-lifting charges as they did in school. It was the first time I had heard the expression, "five finger discount". The children's uncle was addicted to cheap alcohol and would eventually die at forty-one.

## PROTECTING CHILDREN FROM CHILD PROTECTIVE SERVICES

My involvement with the family originally centered around the mother's two elementary school-aged daughters. At that time the state CPS had written off the town of Guadalupe and did not even investigate cases in the area. The local school had become so concerned for the girls they forced CPS to take the girls into protective custody. No Dependency Petition was filed with the Juvenile Court because CPS did not want to get involved with the community and evidence did not exist to substantiate a petition. CPS also wrongly believed they had no authority in Native American communities. They failed to realize the Indian Child Welfare Act only applies to reservations, not to barrios in the city.

As the tribe could take jurisdiction from state CPS, I was phoned on a Friday afternoon by the CPS Worker that she would have to return the children on Monday morning if I did not take custody of them on Monday. When I met the girls, the older pretended she did not understand English. She pointed to a soda machine and I gave her a fifty cent piece to put in the machine. She soon returned and blew her cover by asking if I had two quarters. As with the school teacher and CPS Worker, I was sucked in and I began a journey that helped form the basic reason for writing this book.

The mother was deeply concerned for the welfare of her children but felt there was no future for them. She was clearly overwhelmed, but she never resisted working with me to insure her daughters would have help and hope to break the cycle. The mother had a long history of drug usage, periods of incarceration, and severe medical problems associated with drug usage. She had an inner spiritual strength that belied her outward appearance. It is a prime example of being able to find the good in people if time is taken to uncover it. During her few remaining years I was struck by the strong bond her children had with her, and how hard she was willing to work toward saving them from the life she had endured.

In the state CPS believing the ICWA prevented their taking custody of Native American children, it was demonstrated how few people understand the ICWA. There was and is a substantial need in this town but CPS turned its back on these children and allowed them to become disenfranchised. Not even the tribe wanted to accept their jurisdiction should go beyond the reservation boundary. CPS administrators knew the problems existing in that community. They should have reached out a hand and set up a meeting with town officials and the tribal chairman to work together to provide services to families in Guadalupe. CPS might have established an office in the community, hired and trained Native Americans to work as CPS investigators, and provided the same opportunities they provide to the general public - - working with families in the community or removing children to protect them from themselves. A dialogue must be established to insure a legitimate relationship exists between tribal administrators and state agencies to include CPS. It is not merely to improve quality of life but to save children and help them reach their full potential. Had this family been identified years ago, treatment programs would have curtailed the insidious problems that went unrecognized and unattended for too many years. If a non-court type caseload had been instituted in this community, this and other families could have been provided the kind of treatment programs and monitoring needed to redirect their lives. It is not good enough to say that they should have known better or have changed their own lives.

# CHAPTER THIRTEEN

# CONCLUSION

CPS needs Workers to empathize with families. By empathize I mean understanding that a family's predicament does not infer an inability to rectify the problem with some assistance. We want to encourage a parent to trace the problem back to the cause, help him to identify that cause and encourage him to solve his own problem. Instead of coming across as having all the answers, an investigator must be patient and gather the information from the parent to base a sound decision. The

Worker must closely evaluate whether abuse has been occurring over a long period of time or is it related to a one-time situation that could not be resolved amicably. The manner in which case managers treat families is dictated from the top down. Empathy is a difficult concept in protective services because the normal response to abuse is punitive. Administrators are not willing to jeopardize their job by allowing Workers to indulge in empathy. Workers can be trusted to differentiate between long-term abuse and situational abuse. Empathy can be used to effectively create a treatment program focusing on the problem areas and eliciting the willingness of the parent to participate in a treatment program that is relevant to the problem.

Too often investigations are undertaken with the Worker's mind already made up. By failing to consult with the child's caretaker the Worker fails to receive an accurate view of the family. Instead of listening, Workers pass judgment too quickly. As the parent feels he is understood by the investigator, the parent will become more amenable to a specific treatment program if it is explained how it will address the cause and reason for the problem. Treatment becomes goal oriented. It is simplified to a specific task. The treatment program begins to take over with an intact family. The Worker begins to lengthen the frequency of his visits with the family. Periodically the three member team, parent, Worker, and treatment program, meets to review the progress of treatment. Now CPS has built trust in the parent to phone the next time stress threatens the family stability. Today families do not ever want to see CPS again once treatment is over. CPS should be a resource for parents.

The report by federal investigators has already found 45 out of 45 states failed to adequately provide services to children and families. The commissioner overseeing the review wants to see what is happening to children and families. What is the child welfare practice? Are the children and families moving in the system? Are cases being reviewed in a timely manner? Are visits being made?

This approach may still fall short unless the commissioner requires CPS open random files instead of specific ones designed to place their services in a good light. The federal investigators need to interview the children removed from their home, the parents or primary

133

caretaker, and extended family members. A fair and just review must not rest with the "professionals" cited in this book. It must also evaluate the progression from the Initial Hearing to evaluating psychological evaluations for balance, to frequency of visits, the parent and child interaction during their visits, and culminating in a review of the quality of legal representation for parents and children.

Similar to AA's twelve-step program, CPS cases should follow a similar program:

Step 1: Verifying an Allegation

Interview parents at their home, observe how the home is furnished, and listen carefully for information on the causes of the problem. Interview teachers, doctors, extended family and neighbors as appropriate.

Step 2.: Removal of child(ren)

Request help from the parent in identifying an extended family member to take care of the child. Take parent and child to the placement with family member.

Step 3. Placement of Child

Involve child and parent in accumulating all the child's treasures. Have parent assist in placing child in car or take parent along with child.

Step 4. Arrange Visits

Set up visits for the month with the child's involvement if possible. Increase number of visits if child placed with relative.

Step 5. First Court Hearing

Judge sets tone for court hearings. Notifies he will meet in chambers with parent and child together. Each subsequent hearing he meets with just child and child's attorney.

Step 6. Appropriateness of Treatment

Develop treatment program with parent and parent's attorney present. Nothing should be done without attorney present.

Step 7. Punitive vs. Non-Judgmental

Reinforce goal of being non-judgmental. Allow a chance for treatment program to work.

Be supportive when parent deserves it. Allow parent to read Progress Report.

Step 8. Unbiased Professional Services

All treatment programs and evaluations must avoid presenting a biased picture of the family. Search for good points in the parent. Be honest in the strength of bond between parent and child.

Step 9. Increased Visitation to Overnight Stays

Do not hold child in out-of-home placement until his return. Start process of return through weekend and holiday visits. Observe child during his overnight visit. Does he go back to foster home willingly?

Step 10. Involve Judge in Case Progress

When case moves significantly forward as toward overnight visits, request judge commend parent for significant progress.

Step 11. Return Child in 6-8 Months

Don't drag case on if children are desirous of reuniting. If concerns still exist institute in-home counseling with the child in the home.

Step 12. Graduation Ceremony

Consider the final court hearing as a graduation ceremony. Don't be afraid to give family members a hug.

The 12-step approach pertains to that 30% of cases that fall in the gray area of abuse. Cases of severe physical and sexual abuse do not fall under this purview. Hopefully we can avoid classifying every referral as guilty until proven innocent. Law enforcement has the expertise to question children in cases of abuse. As Social Workers let's remain as a resource to families and children in helping them develop competence and motivation to identify and solve their own problems.

# ABOUT THE AUTHOR

Mr. Schwartz was on his way to becoming a high school teacher and counselor, when he accepted a counselor and team leader position in President Lyndon Johnson's MODEL CITIES PROGRAM, which was an effort to improve the disadvantaged residents and neighborhoods of certain selected cities. The three year program was expanded to five years and Mr. Schwartz was awarded a Citizen of the Year commendation by the mayor. He then transferred to a client advocacy position with the state agency, in which he assisted people facing unexpected and sometimes life-altering catastrophic changes in their lives to find satisfactory resolution to their problems.

Subsequently Mr. Schwartz accepted a Child Protective Services position in working with families to achieve reunification. It was here that his previous view of federal programs as a safety net for families now fostered a punitive and mistrustful approach to families and children. In its attempt to build an empire, CPS conscripted Social Workers, attorneys and the Juvenile Court to deny a fair and just treatment program for family reunification and preservation. Mr. Schwartz completed his career with nine years as a lead investigator of abuse referrals on a Native American reservation. There he expanded CPS to provide rehabilitative services to teenagers caught up in gang activity.

www.ingramcontent.com/pod-product-compliance
Lightning Source LLC
Chambersburg PA
CBHW020433290526
45785CB00002B/828